THE EL　　　　　　　　　　　　TH

R. J. Stewart is a Scottish author and composer who has worked, researched and written extensively on the western esoteric tradition. He has composed and recorded music for television, film, and stage, and is the designer and player of the 80 stringed concert psaltery.

THE ELEMENTS OF

CREATION MYTH

R J Stewart

ELEMENT BOOKS

First published in 1989 by
Element Books Limited
Longmead, Shaftesbury, Dorset

Designed by Jenny Liddle
Illustrations by Stuart Littlejohn
Cover design by Max Fairbrother
Cover illustration by Martin Rieser

Typeset by Selectmove Ltd. London
Printed and bound in Great Britain by
Billings, Hylton Road, Worcester

British Library Cataloguing in Publication Data
Stewart, R. J. (Robert J) 1949–
The elements of creation myth.
1. Myths. Special subjects: Creation
I. Title
291.2'4

ISBN 1-85230-106-6

CONTENTS

ILLUSTRATIONS

THE
INCANTATION

1. In the beginning the Spirit of All-Being
   Becomes breath within the Void,
   And utters forth Four Sounds of Power
   Through Seven Gates of One Creation.
   Each Sound proclaims a Name re-echoing
   Its Origin in Spirit.
   In each Name breath of One Being lives
   Yet each itself becomes a being,
   Four in One
   United by One Sound.

   Know that at the height and depth
   Of Seven levels of Creation
   Two faces of one truth are found –
   One the Father of the Stars
   One the Mother of the Deep,
   United and conjoined forever
   In the Living Child of Light.

2. In the Name of the Star Father
   The Child of Light passes to and fro
   Within without the utter Void.
   He speaks His Word between Two Dragons –
   One reaching to extremity of night and depth,

One reaching to extremity of day and height.
One is coiling time and space
One is coiling power and stars;
Weaving together they enfold the Void
Which draws the heart of Being In and Out.

Through their enfoldment of the Void
The Bright One passes to and fro
According to his will:
As a breath of Air
As a tongue of Fire
As a drop of Water
As a Crystal, clear and perfect.

3. It is in His Name
   That peace is now declared,
   It is in His Name that power is now declared:
   I am a Light and a Keeper of Lights
   I am a Mask of the Bright One
   I bring Light unto the Darkness
   And Darkness to the Light.
   In me are all guardians kings and priests
   Partaking of the Mystery of Weaving;
   The Keys and Keystones are my Knowledge
   The Stars and Starstones are my Wisdom
   The Bright One is my Understanding
   On the Hanging Tree
   Reversed through space and time.

4. In the Name of the Great Mother
   I speak now as Guardian of the Threshold
   Where Light and Dark weave together;
   My Right Hand is a black devouring serpent
   My Left Hand is a bright flaming serpent
   My heart is a wheel of crystal fire
   My feet transform the secret waiting earth
   My brow reveals the Eye of Light, all-seeing.

   Behold the Mystery of the Star Father
   Behold the Mystery of the Deep Mother
   Behold their Being One in Light.

5. Water falls upon the earth
    And seed becomes growing grain;
    Corn becomes bread
    Bread becomes body
    Body becomes crystal
    Through the power of the secret Fire.
    Water becomes wine
    Wine becomes blood
    Blood becomes starlight
    Starlight becomes spirit
    Spirit becomes crystal
    Through the power of the secret earth.

    This is the body of spirit
    In a most perfect form –
    The breath of life is upon it
    The star fire of light lives within it,
    Like unto like across the Void.
    Breath and Light
    Blood and body
    Stars in Worlds
    Bright One in Earth.

    His the Right Hand
    His the Left Hand
    His the Rainbow Letters
    Spiralled in most perfect dragon form:
    Not Seven but Four
    Not Four but Two
    Not Two but One
    In One Being unity
    Unbeing . . . AMEN

R.J. Stewart 1987

THE SONG
OF AMAIRGEN

I am Wind on Sea
I am Ocean Wave
I am Roar of Sea
I am Bull of Seven Battles
I am Vulture on Cliff
I am Dewdrop,
I am Fairest of Flowers
I am Boar for Boldness
I am Salmon in Pool
I am Lake on Plain . . .
I am a Word of Skill,
I am the Point of Weapon (pouring forth combat)
I am the God who forms Fire for the Head.
Who smooths the ruggedness of mountain?
Who announces the ages of the Moon?
And who, the place where sunset will fall?
Who calls the cattle from the House of Tethra?
On whom do the cattle of Tethra smile?
Who is the troop, who the God that sharpens edges?
Enchantments of spear? Enchantments of Wind?

(Ancient Irish poem from the *Lebor Gabâla Érenn* or
Book of Invasions)

INTRODUCTION

This is not a book on comparative mythology or anthropology. No attempt has been made, therefore, to give detailed scientific comparisons of myths and cultures around the world. It is, in fact, a very different kind of book, and even if it had been possible to expand significantly beyond the present limited size, it would not have wandered down the thorny and complex routes of comparative mythology or anthropology, both of which are detailed academic disciplines in their own right. Some of the literature generated by these disciplines is listed in the Bibliography. Nor is this a study of mystical or religious texts in the grand tradition of detailed textual analysis. Thus when texts are quoted the translations need not be regarded as definitive, but merely as working examples drawn from a combination of reasonably authoritative and efficient sources.

This book is an introductory essay on creation mythology, concentrating specifically on cosmography or cosmology ... in other words, the myths concerning the very beginnings of the universe and of our own world. In most books on mythology the creation myths are covered in the initial stages before proceeding to the lives of gods, goddesses and heroes, which tend to take up the interest and efforts of mythographers and scholars.

1

Thus narrative, religious, and sociopolitical matters form the bulk of most texts on mythology. If we concentrate specifically on creation myths, however, we find that they form a very specific and coherent body in their own right, and are not, as is often assumed, mere adjuncts or introductions to the appearance of deities and human societies.

Although creation myths are inevitably embedded within formal religion, they are by no means exclusive to any church, cult, religion, or school of thought. We tend to think of creation stories and mythology as being the product of past cultures, but this is only one part of the picture. Many creation myths are included, or perhaps we might say regenerated, in specialised mystical, magical or metaphysical texts, without necessarily being plagiarised or forged from earlier sources in literature. Thus while most of the quotations or examples in this book are indeed from ancient cultures, or from the living descendants of such cultures today, a few are from more recent sources which, in the present context, help to demonstrate concepts of creation mythology.

To present creation mythology in a short text is not, of course, a straightforward task. I had originally intended to quote a number of examples from different cultures and traditions worldwide, and then present a running, and dare I say it, comparative, commentary upon them. This approach soon proved to be inherently antagonistic to the nature of creation mythology, and to cause loss of sight of the wood through the act of counting trees. It proved more productive to ramble through various quotes and examples as required, but always working from certain previously defined models which are described in detail in later chapters.

My basic thesis is this: creation mythology emerges from certain states of consciousness, from apprehensions of the universe communicated through visual symbols, poetry, and, in the earliest forms of sacred tales, chants, or epics, through music. The myths are not 'explanations' but resonant re-creations that echo the original creation.

If you are certain with an immovable and rigid certainty that creation mythology is simply a crude method of explaining phenomena or disposing of problems concerning the nature of things prior to modern technology, then perhaps you should read no further. If you are of this disposition but do indeed read on, I would suggest that it is worth trying some of the imaginative exercises mentioned briefly below, for their effectiveness is not related to our personal understanding or intellectual appreciation or rejection of mythology in general.

Having selected certain models of creation which occur worldwide, given examples, and discussed their potency or validity, we must next approach the question as to their value for the present day. Clearly they are not valid either as explanations of dogmatic religious beliefs or as scientific facts, and no time is wasted in this book on detailed criticism of any state or national religion or any scientific model of the universe. If creation myths are of any value, it must be found in their magical, poetic, visionary, or psychological potential.

It seems only reasonable for the reader to experiment with this suggestion, and for those with some interest in meditation and visualisation, a few basic exercises based upon the elements of creation mythology have been included in Part Two. Such exercises originally formed part of the detailed training of magicians, seers, priests and priestesses in the context of many other arts and disciplines, but these simple modern variants have been intentionally separated from the more complex and often daunting teachings and traditions.

Curious as it may seem, meditation and visualisation based upon creation mythology does not require belief in the truth of the creation myth concerned: belief is quite irrelevant. If the sequences of the myth, which usually involve coming into existence out of void, and then setting out certain definitions of space, life, and time within the newly defined field of awareness (being), are followed through carefully, they have some surprising results. Rather than giving deep cosmic insights (though this may occur in certain cases) creation myths can and often do have a regenerative and insight-bestowing effect upon the group or individual who uses them actively within the imagination.

In other words, if we imagine the creation of the world, we recreate or rebalance ourselves. This is the foundation of all mystical and magical arts, but in this book we go no further than actual creation myths and their essentially simple but powerful constituent elements. There is no demand upon the reader that he or she be, or seek to become, a mystic, metaphysician, seer, or magician, merely that an interest in the contents and potential of creation mythology be applied in simple visualisation or meditation. As all myths come from oral tradition, from tales or chants told aloud, the exercises are really a modern restatement of the ancient art of empowered or mythic story-telling. And we know or remember from childhood how effective fairy tales can be.

SEEKING ORIGINS BEYOND EXPLANATION

In 1642 the Vice-Chancellor of Cambridge University, Dr Lightfoot, proclaimed that the world was created at 9 am on 23 October 4004 BC. This polished and dogmatically refined system of dating was based upon the slightly earlier work of Archbishop Ussher of Armagh, who had already decided upon the year 4004 BC through his studies and calculations based upon the Old Testament. Such authoritarian statements, heralding in an eccentric way the so-called Age of Reason that was to follow, must seem like childish nonsense to the modern reader, yet they are merely episodes in a long series of attempts to date creation, attempts which still endure within modern astronomy and physics. So the details and utterly proven conclusions change as previous theories and 'facts' are discarded, but the urge remains. This urge to reduce the power of a mystery by labelling it, by filing it into a little box assembled from a dogmatic or pre-contrived system, is one of the most dangerous and inherently weakening or disabling aspects of western consciousness. Fortunately it is neither triumphant nor endemic.

There are a small number of child-like but major questions inherent in human awareness; they reach through time and circumstances, culture and history, and enormous efforts are made either to bury such questions altogether or to capitalise and profit from the administration of dogmatic answers. In mythic or poetic terms, each age or culture provides the type of answer that it deserves, and benefits or suffers thereby.

The pedantic seventeenth-century dating of the moment of creation gradually led to the even more stultifying pomposities of the Higher or Historic Criticism, beloved of Victorian divines, in which exact meanings were ascribed to orthodox scripture. This pernicious nonsense, strange to say, somehow paved the way for Darwin's theory of evolution. Darwin's work was deadly to the already decaying state religion, yet was the direct product of western culture's obsession with rational reductive thought and detailed labelling of events into series or chains of cause and effect. Both the Higher Criticism and Darwin's theory are the products of rampant materialism, and run quite contrary to the deep stream of mythic tradition and mythic history which produced the great philosophers, thinkers, civilisations and arts and sciences of the ancient world.

The mystery of creation is not a problem to be solved either through dogma or logical or even evolutionary systems; it may only be approached through altogether other levels of consciousness. These are the levels found in mythology, which speak directly to the imagination in a primordial language of timeless imagery and potent, potentially transformative, narrative. The child-like questions, such as where does the sun go at night, where are the stars, who was the first man or woman, are not answered by myth; there is a common fallacy that myths were devised as answers to questions beyond the comprehension of ancient humanity, dealing in an ignorant superstitious manner with problems that could only be finally resolved by modern science. As part of a living culture, however, myths provided an organic timeless flow of images and narratives within which such questions were by-passed altogether, for the 'answers' of mythology come from deep levels of consciousness, in which universal patterns or intimations are apprehended.

The declaration or recounting of a myth is, at its deepest and most powerful level, a reverberation of the event which it describes. Thus myths are not allegories but resonances or reflections of actualities, of occurrences or manifestations at the heart of being.

Why should we be concerned with beginnings? The interest has had a revival in each century; our twentieth-century revival has been triggered by rampant material-ism and exploitation of world resources; people are sickened by the blatant corruption within which they are forced to live, and so turn to alternative modes of thought, ways of life, points of view, often simply as a trivial escape, but sometimes in a sincere and disciplined manner. So we have a paradox; in a culture in which myth and legend have been ruthlessly destroyed and trivialised, we have an ever growing interest in mythology, legendary history, and the resulting esoteric arts and sciences which were linked to myth and legend inseparably by our ancestors.

Such interest is not simply a type of juvenile pseudo-revolutionary revival; people realise intuitively that if they lose contact with the key images within myth, or with mythic patterns, they will lose contact with a reality that both underpins and transcends the superficiality of our civilisation. Thus myth may be approached as a means of regeneration, both for the individual and for the larger group. In a magical or metaphysical sense, the utterance of creation myth is a resonance of the actual creation of the world, or of the universe. A famous verse from Fitzgerald's *Rubáiyát of Omar Khayyám* is not merely wishful thinking or romantic yearning:

Ah Love! could thou and I with Fate conspire

> To grasp this sorry Scheme of Things entire,
> Would we not shatter it to bits – and then
> Re-mould it nearer to the Heart's Desire!

Fitzgerald/Khayyám states in what are, initially, romantic terms, one of the great mythic, mystical, and magical truths: if we are able to understand our world through its inherent patterns, then we might be able to 'remould it nearer to the Heart's Desire'. By this the poet means nearer to a divine conception, archetype, or spiritual reality and not a personal romantic or sensuous end. Although myths are essentially anonymous, many mythic spiritual truths are found in great poetry, particularly when the poet draws upon or taps into an established mythic tradition, as in our example.

PART ONE

CREATION MYTHOLOGY

1. CREATION MYTHOLOGY

What is creation mythology? Before we can answer the question, we must first try to define an answer to another equally important one: what is mythology? As the main thesis of this book is that creation mythology is the foundation for all mythology, we need a clear definition of myth before proceeding. The definition which is used in this book is as follows:

A myth is a story embodying and declaring a pattern of relationship between humanity, other forms of life, and the environment. This may seem fairly straightforward and agreeable, but it has many implications extending far beyond a materialist or psychological definition and interpretation of myth. Let us examine the definition in more detail, as it divides naturally into three parts.

1. *A myth is a story.* Myths are found initially in oral tradition: this means that they are tales handed down by word of mouth and preserved collectively and anonymously, though specific story-tellers or creative poets and writers often work with them. The earliest known literary use of the word myth is in the works

of Plato where *mythologia* is used to mean the telling of tales customarily containing legendary characters such as gods, goddesses, heroes, and revered ancestors.

Most traditional myths come to us in a literary form from an early cultural period, as texts forming a watershed between oral tradition and written dogma or history. In a few rare but important cases, we may find living examples of myth in oral tradition, either from people who still live in a relatively primal or underdeveloped cultural state (by comparison to the rapidly changing technological world) or from living oral tradition still found, in a few places, within developed societies, usually in isolated regions where twentieth-century advances are present but have not totally erased traditional culture.

As a myth is a story, and there is a false emphasis upon 'facts' being vitally important in our society, we have the rather confusing and enervating modern concept that anything illusory, fantastical or downright untrue is a 'myth'. This is an unfortunate misconception, as it tends to cloud our understanding of true myth, which can express many *facts*, or more significantly *truths* in an emblematic, poetic or visionary manner which is most efficient and effective, and often more communicative than many thousands of highly reasoned words or rigid formulae. Myths reveal their content to other levels of awareness than the merely logical or reasoning mental processes; in some cases they can leap beyond these processes altogether to convey truth.

The *Oxford English Dictionary* defines myth as a purely fictitious narrative usually involving supernatural persons, actions, or events, and embodying some popular idea concerning natural or historical phenomena. The dictionary then adds that the word 'myth' is often used vaguely to indicate any narrative with fictitious elements. So the dictionary definition is not so different from that used as the basis of this book . . . or is it? To grasp the difference we should examine the second of the three constituent parts of our working definition.

Thank you for choosing this book.
If you would like to receive regular
information about Element titles,
please fill in this card.

Please tick the subjects that are of particular
interest to you

- [ ] PHILOSOPHY
- [ ] HEALTH & HEALING
- [ ] BUDDHISM, TAOISM
- [ ] WOMEN'S STUDIES
- [ ] EARTH MYSTERIES
- [ ] NEW SCIENCE
- [ ] CHRISTIANITY
- [ ] MYTHOLOGY
- [ ] YOGA

- [ ] ANCIENT WISDOM, ASTROLOGY, TAROT
- [ ] NATIVE AMERICAN
- [ ] HINDUISM
- [ ] QABALAH
- [ ] FICTION
- [ ] PSYCHOLOGY
- [ ] SUFISM, ISLAM
- [ ] WESTERN MYSTERY TRADITION

Other subjects of interest . . . .

. . . .

Name . . . .

Address . . . .

. . . .

. . . .

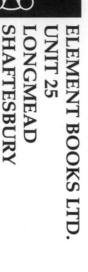

ELEMENT BOOKS LTD.
UNIT 25
LONGMEAD
SHAFTESBURY
DORSET SP7 8BR

2. A myth *embodies and declares* a pattern or patterns of relationship. This aspect of myth should be given very careful attention. The dictionary definition states that a myth 'embodies some popular idea concerning natural or historical phenomena', but the content of myth, and its relationship to collective tradition (from which popular ideas are generated) is often far more subtle than that of a mere narrative.

The unfolding or declaration of any myth includes sequences, structures and relationships, which form very specific and recognisable patterns; these are often called *mythic* patterns. The pattern of relationship in a myth, particularly if it is part of a sequence deriving from a primal or enduring tradition with roots deep in early human history, is often a narrative and, more significantly, a *visual* exposition of specific concepts. These concepts are expressed as tales or verses concerning magic, metaphysics, energies of life and death, or of creation and dissolution. We shall return to this visual quality of myth again, but for the moment it simply means that myths are energised not only by the events and characters of the narrative, but by the effect that they have upon our imagination, by their ability to be expressed, accepted, retained and enjoyed, as images, as pictures.

The traditional formulae of myths, which are the roles and appearance of certain characters, many of which are known in parallel forms worldwide, and the specific language and rhythms of delivery used by a story-teller (originally), also act directly upon the deeper levels of our consciousness. Such elements, the visual and the rhythmic, in which rhythm includes not only song or verse but the pace and structure of the narrative and its interacting characters, all contribute to the effect of the mythic patterns.

There are a small number of what may be called master maps or glyphs, upon which many myths may be located and interpreted for educational or meditative purposes. Such glyphs are anonymous, seemingly present in esoteric magical or spiritual traditions from a very early date, and with no originator, inventor, or first copyright appearance. They are formalised presentations of patterns inherent within human consciousness.

Such master glyphs are not individual pictures in the usual sense, but plans upon which the better known mythic images may be unfolded and located in quite clear and often detailed significant relationships to one another. Mythic relationships are often invisible in any one narrative or set of narratives, and tend to work anonymously or unconsciously. This inner level of myth is not fully accommodated by the dictionary definition.

Typical master maps or glyphs, found in various forms worldwide, are those of the Interlinked Worlds (Figure 1), the Tree of Life (Figure 5), the Wheel of Life (Figure 3); typical orders or sets of relationship are found in the pantheons of gods and goddesses, the careers of certain heroes and heroines, the appearances and travels of tribes, races, and specific families, and the relationship between humans and their land, in which orders, castes, geomantic or traditional zones and divisions are preserved from ancient times.

Emblems, symbolic sets of images, and magical alphabets may be added to the master maps; the Tarot is an important western example of such a set of images, as are the signs of the Zodiac and planets, set upon the turning Wheel of the Sky (Figure 4), known in various interrelated versions throughout human history and around the world. The astrology inherent within mythology, however, seems to predate the establishment of a finely calculated art, and be more concerned with direct observation of recurring or remarkable star patterns. We shall return to this fascinating aspect of mythology later.

3. The mythic relationship is between humanity, other forms of life, and the environment. The third part of our working definition might seem initially to correspond

very well to the OED definition, 'concerning natural or historical phenomena', which is preceded by reference to supernatural characters. But the involvement of myth with natural history or cultural history is misleading, for such involvement is a later expansion stretched out upon the foundations of creation mythology.

We can move beyond the explanatory level of interpretation only when we consider that 'the environment' ranges from the immediate locality of a story-teller, through the land, the continent, the planet, the solar system, and ultimately the universe. Myths deal precisely and in depth with both a local and a universal environment; indeed, it is often difficult to separate the two, for the local environment mirrors a universal one, and myth leaps instantaneously from what appear to be localised occurrences to what are, undoubtedly, universal or cosmic events, often using the same characters, symbols, and relationships to define both.

The stellar or astrological content of mythology often works in this way; one moment a character is human, involved in some drama, the next he or she is a stellar entity, clearly related to a pattern of stars or planets found in the sky at a certain time of year. This paradoxical role of myth was rationalised by the Ancient Greeks, when they stated that their heroes were placed among the stars by the gods as reward for their valour or service.

The master maps referred to above act as connecting or interfacing structures between the environment of earth, our planetary and human realm, and the world of the stars, planets, and ultimately the universe. Divine personae, gods and goddesses, and other life forms, also inhabit this total environment. On the deepest level of all, the environment is not only one of space, energy and time, but of consciousness, which unifies those three into one, and from which, according to ancient tradition, all other forces and forms were generated. To imagine, therefore, is to echo the original creation of the universe.

Figure 1 The Three Worlds

The Three Worlds is a general model of Creation, found in many myths, legends, religions, and in magical and esoteric tradition. It may be used as a map for the study of mythology, upon which characters, events and places may be located.

Both *The Three Worlds* and *The Tree of Life* (Figure 5) are flat representations of spherical conceptual models. Thus the Three Worlds may be interpreted as *harmonics* of one another, three states or conditions or modes of Being within an infinite universal sphere. They may also be seen as three interpenetrating spheres, contained within one overall sphere.

A simpler variant is the Triple Spiral, in which the Three Worlds or levels of the spiral have an apparent hierarchy, one above the other, but are composed of one single entity, the spiralling line. The Triple Spiral is a variant of the spherical model, rather like peeling an apple. The spiralling image is frequently found in association with the *Axis Mundi* or World Pivot, represented as a pole, tree, spindle or distaff, reaching through all three worlds, acting as their central binding or empowering instrument. The Triple Spiral is wound from the thread attached to the distaff or spindle (see Plato's *Myth of Er the Armenian*, page 83)

Definitions of the Three Worlds vary considerably in world mythology, but certain patterns are consistent. A general definition might be as follows:

1. **Stellar World:** Stars (and Sun, sometimes Planets of Solar System) / occupied by Creator and other supreme deities or transcendent entities, spirits, forces.

2. **Planetary World:** Earth (sometimes Moon and Planets) / occupied by Humanity, Animals, and Plants: also by orders of spirits and elemental entities.

3. **Underworld:** within the planet, or as a realm of proto-matter and primal power / occupied by chthonic beings, ancestral spirits, mineral and elemental entities, titanic and amorphous deities and forces.

Many entities are natural to specific worlds and do not move beyond them: others, however, have freedom to move through the worlds at will, while some may act as contacts or messengers between adjoining worlds.

The triple division may be further simplified into:

1. **Sky World:** that which is above (the realm of the Star or Sky Father in primal myth and legend).

2. **Earth World or Land:** that which is visible to the horizon by turning a full circle (the realm of humanity and the goddess / god of the Land).

3. **Underwold:** that which is unknown beneath (the realm of the ancestors and the Great Goddess).

Each of the Three Worlds may reflect a triple pattern, manifesting a *Ninefold Creation*: this is the basis of the *Tree of Life*. Thus the Stellar World was often divided into three zones in ancient mythic astronomy, giving Three Zones or Worlds. This pattern is still the basis of modern astrology, but should not be confused with it, as there are many significant and substantial differences between mythic astronomy and modern mathematical (i.e. non-observational) astrology. (See page 36–8 for a more detailed summary.)

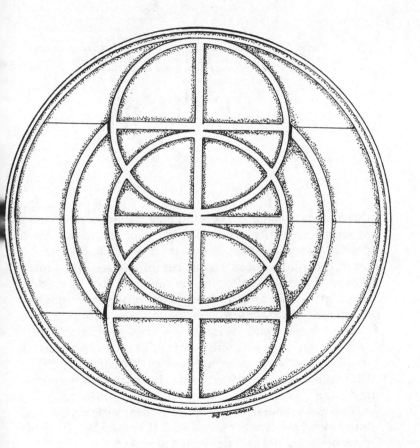

2. MODELS OF CREATION

If we examine the range of creation mythology, we find that the statements concerning creation are not arbitrary or wildly varied. While it would be foolish to lay down precise analytical rules when it comes to any aspect of myth, let alone those sequences of images and words that re-utter the creation of the universe and its worlds, or of our planet and its living beings, we may consider some preliminary definitions, models or working systems. These are not rigid inflexible models, in the scientific sense of requiring specific proofs or of providing answers to questions. Myth does not seek to answer questions in the manner required by modern science, but is a perpetual re-telling, re-creation, of the great story of existence.

Two main models seem to prevail in creation mythology: for convenience in this short book they may be called the directional model and the image model.

THE DIRECTIONAL MODEL

In the directional model, creation is allocated to specific directions which manifest out of the void or abyss. This may be a fairly simple allocation, or it may become a highly developed mathematical and topological model, as in the philosophy and metaphysics of the Kabbalah, which is, nevertheless, based upon some very simple primal creation theories. The famous ancient creation verses of the *Sepher Yetzirah* rooted deeply in Jewish esoteric tradition (see page 75) are a classic example of the directional model.

But such models were not confined to mystical vision or obscure tuition, for we find that the cosmic map was quite intentionally mirrored in the physical organisation of ancient cultures. Cities, regions, entire lands, were appointed directions, quarters allocated to certain forces and qualities in the ancient world. From India to Ireland may seem a huge cultural and geographical leap, yet even such distant lands shared the common heritage of the Six Directions as actual zones in the land; East, South, West, North, Above, and Below. Civilisations and cultures allocated their landscapes, skills, tribes, castes, and activities accordingly. Nor was the concept confined to the Indo–European peoples, of which the Celts and the races of India are part. We find it in distinctly oriental cultures, with versions in China, for example, dating back thousands of years.

The directional structure of society was rooted in creation myth, and was not originally political; indeed, ancient patterns persisted until relatively recent times, in direct distinction from accumulated religious or political divisions or developments. Certain hierarchical social systems are connected to the directional model of creation myth, for when the land is set out according to the four directions of east, south, west, and north, with the starry and sky divinities above, and the underworld and earth powers below, humanity forms a middle zone or tier within the

Figure 2 The Six Directions

The Six Directions model is essential to the understanding of creation mythology, and to mythology in general. This deceptively simple pattern, based upon the concepts of *consciousness, perception* and *relativity*, underpins mythology from the simplest primal story of creation to the sophisticated metaphysics of Eastern religions or the Kabbalah and other mystical systems which describe and reflect universal creation.

The Directions are principally based upon the relative potential status or concepts of direction of a human being standing upright: *Above, Below, Before, Right, Left, Behind.* But in creation myth, this physical relativity, the human form, is only a reflection or harmonic of an original or divine setting out of Six Universal Directions: *Above, Below, East, South, North,* and *West.* While the human directions are limited by horizons (visual limits) the metaphysical directions are limitless, and may also be employed in the human imagination to perceive beyond the visual horizons.

The relative planetary zones of East, South, North, and West, are of course defined by the apparent position of the Sun, by the planetary orbit, and by magnetic fields. But they may be extended into the solar system, stellar space, or to a universal pattern. In each of the three cases, *human, planetary, universal,* a sphere is defined, either literal (around an entity) or apparent (of relative definition), or metaphysical/astronomical. This triplication corresponds to the concept of the *Three Worlds* (see Figure 1).

Many ancient cultures were organically and hierarchically divided into zones according to the Six Directions, giving a three-dimensional strata to a land and its inhabitants: certain skills and arts were found, located, and traditionally encouraged in territories in each of the Four Directions (East, South, North, West) while the vertical strata reflected the hierarchy of the Three Worlds. In ancient Ireland, for example, the royal court was in the centre of the land, with the Four Provinces surrounding it, each having specific arts, skills, functions, and traditional roles. In a simple sense this persisted even into medieval European culture, with the triple division of Royalty, Nobility, People, which, though greatly abused and corrupted, reflects very ancient caste systems with an originally mythic rather than political significance.

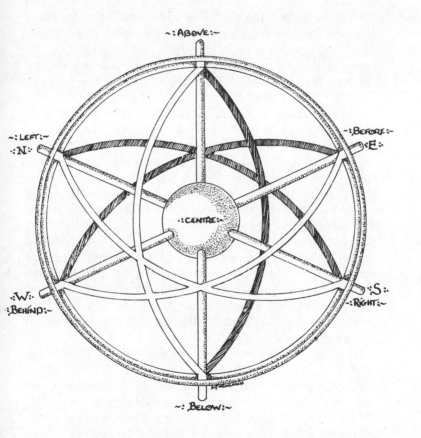

three-dimensional sphere of existence.

THE IMAGE MODEL

This might also be called the anthropomorphic model, for in most cases it involves creation taking the image of human form. In some myths and legends, other creatures form the image with humanity appearing at a later stage. The image model is usually closely related to the directional model, for a human body standing upright upon the face of the planet, automatically defines the primary directions (see Figure 2).

Thus we must be careful never to assume that ancient philosophers truly demanded that we believe the universe to be a giant male or female body ... this would be too simplistic. The image models, however, do attribute certain relationships or harmonic correspondences between parts of the human body and phases of creation of the universe. In both Classical and Renaissance magic and alchemy one of the prime axioms was the ancient hermetic teaching 'as above so below', the microcosm of humanity being a lesser world which reflected and embodied in miniature the macrocosm or greater world of the universe. Sometimes a 'mediacosm', if we may coin a word, is inherent in such patterns, this being the body or entity of the solar system – with sun, planets, and overall sphere of energy.

One key to both the image model and the directional model is in the concept of *entities*. The universe, the solar system, the planet Earth, and humanity, are considered to be entities which partake of one another: they grow out of one another, are reflections of one another, and have a harmonic or holographic relationship within one another.

In many examples, the directional or topological model and the image or anthropomorphic model are fused together. The image model frequently employs a tree, as in the Norse World Tree Yggdrasil, or the Kabbalistic and Biblical Tree of Life (see Figures 5 and 6); it may revolve around a mountain, as in the universal Mount Meru that is the pivot of all worlds in Hindu and Buddhist metaphysics.

The following Brahmanic creation poem fuses the image of a deity with the concept of the universal directions: it is thus a combination of the image model and the directional model:

The Laws of Manu Chapter One

This world was darkness unknowable without form, beyond reason and perception as if utterly asleep.

Then the august and self-existent Being, he who never unfolded, having unfolded this universe under the form of the great elements and others, having shown his energy, appeared to scatter the shades of darkness.

This Being whom only the spirit can perceive, subtle, without distinct parts, eternal, including in himself all creatures, incomprehensible, appeared spontaneously.

Wishing to draw different creatures from his body, he first by thought produced the waters and deposited his seed in them.

This seed became a golden egg as brilliant as the sun, in which he himself was born in the form of Brahmâ, the first father of all worlds.

The waters are called Nârâs, they are the daughters of Nara, and since they were his first dwelling-place (ayana) he took the name Nârâyana.

From this first cause, indistinct, eternal, including in itself being and not-being, came the Male (principle), known in the world by the name of Brahmâ.

In this egg the blessed one remained a whole year, then of himself, by the effort of thought alone, he divided the egg into two parts.

From the two parts he made heaven and earth, and between them the air, the eight cardinal points, and the eternal abode of the waters.

From himself he drew forth the Spirit, including in itself being and not-being, and from the Spirit he drew the feeling of selfhood which is conscious of personality and is master.

And also the great principle of the Soul, and all objects which possess the three qualities, and successively the five organs of the senses which perceive material things.

(Brahmanic creation myth, found in various translations.)

To the image and directional models, we might add the vibratory and ladder models. These are really offshoots of the first two: the vibratory model is, perhaps, more scientific in its precise application of metaphysics to physics. It is found in those various myths in which sound as a sacred force generates the words. Sometimes the sound is uttered by the primal deity, but it may also be all-pervasive, and generate the gods and goddesses out of itself. In Plato's Myth of Er (see Chapter 11), a fusion of cosmology and a vibratory model is made, in a manner that has bedevilled would-be 'precise' thinkers and mathematicians since it was rediscovered after the Dark Ages.

The ladder model is a very simple reduction of the more subtle concepts of spherical universe and directional creation. This simply shows a vertical pattern, with heaven and the blessed at the top, and hell and the cursed at the bottom. It is, in fact, the Axis Mundi, pivot of the worlds, of the ancient perennial philosophy, but wrenched out of its proper context. It is interesting to note that the more militant religions tend towards simplistic models, while those with a contemplative nature or less aggressive attitude retain in full the ancient traditions of complex cosmology.

Even a serial mythic creation progression, however, may be used to reach towards deeper levels of understanding or enlightenment. One of the methods used in early training in both Eastern and Western traditions, is to pass through a series of realms, worlds, or states of manifestation, moving progressively towards higher or primal undifferentiated entities, each of which subsumes the one before it. The Western version of this meditative or imaginative method is frequently cosmological, reaching from the Earth, through the realms of Moon and Sun, the planets, and out to the stars. This cosmological progression, in meditation and visualisation, triggers a gradually deepening and transformative change of consciousness within the student. The method was clearly described by Plotinus, in an exercise on visualisation which uses creation myth as its source and ultimate aim:

Plotinus, On the Nature of 'Intelligible Beauty' (V.viii. cap.ix., AD 550)

Let us then form a mental image of this cosmos with each of its parts remaining what it is, and yet interpenetrating with one another, imagining them altogether into one as much as we possibly can – so that whatever one comes first into the mind as the 'one', (as for instance, the outermost sphere of fixed stars), there immediately follows also the sight of the semblance of the sun, and together with it that of the other stars or planetary spheres, and the earth and sea, and all things living, as though in one transparent sphere – in fine, as though all things could be seen in it.

Let there then be in the soul some semblance of a sphere of light, having all things in it, whether moving or still, or some of them moving and others still.

And holding this sphere in the mind, conceive within yourself another sphere, removing from it all concept of mass; take from it also the concept of space, and the phantom of matter in your mind; and try not to imagine it merely as another sphere less massive than the former.

Then invoking God who has made the reality of which you hold the phantom in your consciousness, pray that He may come.

And may He come with His own cosmos, with all the gods therein – He being one and all, and each one all, united into one, yet different in their powers, and yet in that one manifold all one.

Nay, rather, the One God in all gods, for that He never falls short of His Self, though all of the others are from Him. And they are all together, yet each again apart, being in a state transcending all extension, and possessed of forms that no sense may perceive.

For otherwise, one would be in one place, another in another, and each would be individual to each, and not All in itself, without parts other from the others and other from itself.

Nor is each whole a power divided and proportioned according to a measurement of parts; but each whole is the All, all power, extending infinitely and infinitely powerful – nay, so vast is the Divine world-order that its very parts are infinite.

(Quoted in G.R.S. Mead, *Quests Old and New*, pp. 160–2.)

An alternative method, frequently used, is to progress from the physical body through various levels of increasingly subtle existence, reaching towards metaphysical unity and original perfection. This is mirrored in many Eastern verses:

The essence of all beings is earth,
the essence of earth is water,
the essence of water is plants,
the essence of plants is humanity,
the essence of humanity is speech,
the essence of speech is sacred poetry,
the essence of sacred poetry is music,
the essence of music is OM
The best of all essences, the highest,
Deserving the highest place, the eighth.

(The Chandogya Upanishad)

3. THE UNKNOWN BEGINNING

Creation mythology acts as the perennial foundation for religion, mysticism, magic, and for general mythology which expands from the opening of creation, the beginning of Being. Although variant expressions of creation myths use different apparatus and personae, there is a similarity to such myths worldwide, which may be very generally summarised as follows:

1. Being commences from an unknown source or condition; Being from Not-Being.

2. The original Being, the oneness of the universe, reflects, divides itself or creates further entities.

3. Out of this further development of Being into beings, the worlds are created. The creation of worlds and beings may be separated intellectually, but traditionally they are simultaneous, as worlds

themselves are beings, and the entities in any world make up that world in its entirety.

This triple pattern is frequently reflected in the mythic definition of three worlds: in a modern presentation we might summarise this as the world of the stars (the universe), the world of the sun, moon, and planets (the solar system) and the world of our planet and all its life forms. The triple division may also have within each of the three worlds or levels a cyclic or spiral fourfold expression, corresponding to the ancient four elements of air, fire, water, and earth (see Figures 1 and 3). In refined mythic and mystical traditions, such as those embodied in the Kabbalah, or in Renaissance magic drawing upon classical sources, the four stages of intensifying or reflecting Being are:

1. origination
2. creation
3. formation
4. expression.

These have a certain affinity or relationship to the cycle of the four elements: 1. air 2. fire 3. water 4. earth (see Figure 3).

The majority of traditional mythologies, however, do not include such overt or technically detailed statements. Nevertheless the stages, worlds, and elements, are frequently present by inference, or, (and this is frequently underestimated or even ignored altogether by modern writers upon mythology), through a general understanding on the part of the story-teller and listener, an understanding which, although it needs explanation to the modern reader, would have been part of a fundamental world-view in its own time and place.

Much of the effect of mythology depends upon the hidden or unspoken parts of tales, and their place within a cultural ambience and in unwritten traditions involving further tales to which they are connected. Thus we always have an incomplete body of myth from early times, because the completion, in a modern sense of a full and comprehensive system collection or series, never existed in its own right. On a more subtle level, the completion of a mythic pattern involves an active contribution from the individual; it arises within our consciousness rather than as an exterior narrative. The tales themselves are echoes of primary energies or patterns, which should, ideally, arouse a similar resonant response within the listener. Myth, therefore, leads to revelation, inspiration, and transformation.

In a mythic pattern, such as the creation of the worlds, tales tell of the appearance of characters, their interaction, and the resulting changes in the world or worlds that arise from their loves, battle, tasks, joys and conflicts. Far from being explanations of matters of geography or history, such primal myths are actual declarations and resonances of the original creation of the worlds. In a more localised sense, they describe the manifestation of the land to which the specific myth belongs. We must always remember that this is frequently a reflection of the creation of the universe; land and universe are part of one another, mutually interacting, interdependent, inseparable.

In Irish legend, for example, we find that the successive races that appeared in the land of Ireland each made specific changes to the land itself: lakes were made, plains levelled, rivers and springs arose, and so forth.

Such topological or topographical matters are not yet concerned with politics or social welfare, as might be inferred from later stages such as introduction of farming, brewing of beer, marriage customs and so forth, but are to do with the overt substance, growth and development of the land itself. Many of the later developments listed, such as agriculture or social customs, are in fact part of the same expanding creation myth, and need not necessarily be part of a historical or pseudo-historical reality at all. Frequently a myth, such as the appearance of the first farmer or brewer, is attached to true historical people, though they may not have been the actual first farmers or brewers, but merely the most recent people to fit the bill, either through the filtering process of collective memory, or more subtly because, as an invading and superior force, they were worked into the enduring organic development myths that spring out of those of original creation.

4. RELIGION AND MYTHIC ASTRONOMY

The foundations of creation mythology are anonymous and protean. Such primal myths are timeless, yet we recognise that they have been handed down to us in various forms from ancient times. This last definition may seem self-contradictory or paradoxical, but it is not inimical to our understanding of creation myth.

There is an important link between the deepest roots of consciousness and the apparent passage of historical time. The word 'apparent' is used deliberately here, for the passage of time is not a constant concept throughout the world's cultures, varying considerably from race to race and, indeed, from century to century. Upon the mythic levels that we are discussing, time is seldom regarded as a straight linear sequence, but more often as a spiral or a series of circular or rotating interactions with space and events. In the vast mythic timeframe of Indian myth and religion for example, cosmological lifetimes are accounted, with the reiteration of new cycles occurring over periods of time that are on a stellar rather than a human scale.

The further back we seem to reach in time, the closer we approximate to deep levels of consciousness often closely concealed and inaccessible within the modern mind. This link is supported by certain aspects of ancient thought, particularly those of cosmology, metaphysics, and spiritual contemplation. Not all aspects or ramifications of ancient culture, however, can be related to levels or modes of consciousness; such an exercise would be pointless and misleading.

The primal subjects of creation myth, however, were tackled by the ancients in a number of ways: they fused myth, astronomy, cosmology and poetic or mystical intuition in a synthesis that is often unacceptable to the modern intellect. It should be emphasised in this context that the viewpoint of the ancients was coherent, organic, and holistic. In other words there was no compartmentalising or rigid separation of myth, astronomy, cosmology, mystical intuition, magic, or religion. This unification does not imply lack of discretion or an undeveloped state of mentation in our ancestors worldwide, but a way of thinking and living that resonated to cycles and values vastly different from our own.

To relate to these early modes of consciousness, we need to attune to such levels deep within ourselves as resonate to the unified or organic world-views. The deepest intimations of reality, found in meditation or contemplation, correspond directly to the ancient tales, cosmographies, and metaphysical patterns handed down to us. Such myths are embodied in folklore, religion, and magical and mystical traditions that have remained outside any orthodox framework, but preserved a recognisable integrity and coherence throughout the centuries.

There is, however, a noticeable difference between the broad expansion of mythology in general, as it developed through cultural history in any land or region, and the primal cosmography of creation myth. In many ways the detailed teachings of mystical and magical traditions are nearer to creation mythology than are, say, the overall collected mythological traditions of any race, region, or religion.

In orthodox religions, despite that accumulation of propaganda and style inevitable in any power structure, there is always an element of creation myth. Religions are founded upon many supports, but the deepest of all is often the creation of the worlds, even when it is thrust into the background of attention or corrupted through political manoeuvering.

We may now return briefly, as promised, to the relationship between mythology and astronomy.

MYTHIC ASTRONOMY

One factor that seems to play an important but confused and misunderstood role in mythology is the role of the stars. It is clear that mythic astronomy, the forerunner of astrology as it is found today, is closely woven into the cloth of mythology in general. Creation myths, furthermore, often seem to speak of a pre-solar or pre-planetary phase of existence in terms which may be likened, albeit in a non-technical and non-mathematical sense, to some of the most recent cosmological theories of modern physics and astronomy.

For many years it was customary to explain mythology as either the social and religious legends of any people, explaining various changes in culture or ruler, or simplistic sets of answers to questions concerning nature, the planets, the stars in the sky. Many ancient myths seemed, superficially, to support this theory, for they stated explicitly that certain heroes were turned into groups of stars visible in the sky, or that major deities were related to planetary forces, which in turn were connected to the appearance of the seven planets over the horizon.

The reductionist theory, that of myths as explanations of the patterns of the stars, is greatly weakened by the simple fact that detailed and accurate astronomical observations were kept by early people. We must therefore balance the

Figure 3 The Wheel of Life

The Wheel of Life is found in many variants worldwide, and may be interpreted in a number of ways which interconnect with one another. Its simplest meaning is that of the Fourfold Cycle of the Year: *Spring, Summer, Autumn, Winter.* Upon this simple cyclical framework, as may be seen from our detailed caption below, an ever-expanding set of correspondences may be defined.

Like the *Six Directions*, of which it comprises a major part, (that of one flat plane, usually but not inevitably, the horizontal one), this emblem of creation is one of *relativity*, and acts as a glyph or map for the life cycle of the universe, from stars to sub-atomic particles.

In Buddhism, the Wheel is frequently employed as a symbol of the cycles of illusion or sensual bondage and rebirth, but on an inner or esoteric level it also holds the keys to liberation. Many of the initiatory secrets of the ancient Mysteries or of religions and magical systems were concerned with liberation from the apparent bondage of the spiralling of the Wheel of Life.

From the Four Elements of *Air / Fire / Water / Earth*, or Four Universal Powers of *Life / Light / Love / Law*, all existence unfolds. In astrology the individual birth chart is assembled from a Circle or Wheel of Twelve Signs and Houses, deriving from the basic Four Elements, within which planets form patterns of relationship (see Figure 4). Mythic astronomy, however, is a pre-astrological system of correspondences found throughout the ancient world, developed through observation of star and planetary movements, and of the cycles of the sun, moon, and seasons. Many creation myths tell of the opening out of the Wheel of Life, or how the Universe expanded from out of Chaos into Four Primal Elements, a pattern which is mirrored right through into material and human creation.

For millennia, medicine was based upon an elemental system, as was all science; in certain specific medical systems, this perennial world-view or conceptual model is still employed. Even modern medicines and sciences may be interpreted according to an Elemental model, though the familiar 'table of elements' in modern physics and chemistry is not related to the ancient system.

1. **East** / Air / Spring / Dawn / Beginning / Birth

2. **South** / Fire / Summer / Noon / Increasing / Adulthood

3. **West** / Water / Autumn / Dusk / Fulfilling / Maturity

4. **North** / Earth / Winter / Night / Concluding / Old Age and Death

Just as all creation was said to be composed of the Four Elements, modern genetics defines all living entities by a fourfold code. Thus genetics is a typical example of the fourfold elemental creation model.

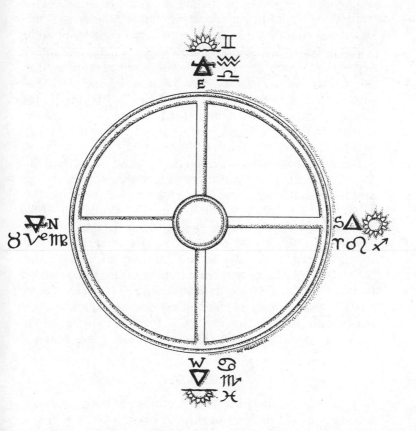

poetic conception of myths with the scientific fact that stars were watched, their motions calculated, and in many cases marked with substantial buildings, alignments, stone monuments and so forth by ancient civilisations. Furthermore, great emphasis was laid upon specific star groupings or patterns of relationship which seem insignificant or even invisible to the modern eye. The Pleiades, a small star group, and the Lunar Nodes which constitute one of the celestial equivalents of those Dragons found in many myths and legends, are significant examples of mythic astronomy. The Pleiades have a mythic and seasonal role in ceremonies practised worldwide, while the Lunar Nodes (Dragon's Head and Tail), though invisible as entities in their own right, have played an important role in astrology since the earliest times.

When we examine creation myths, we find that the earliest levels of creation involve definition of space and directions, after which the stars (above) and the earth (below) may come into being. This process is often reflected through various stages, in which the primal energies, positive and negative, repeat themselves in a series of polarised reflections. Often an old world-order is destroyed to make way for a new one, and this features in many myths and legends. Astronomy plays a significant part in such sequences, for the powers, gods, goddesses, and events within any mythic pattern or tale are often explicitly said to equate to celestial entities or phenomena.

HAMLET'S MILL

A particularly complex and fascinating essay towards understanding this relationship between myth and celestial patterns, has been assembled in the book *Hamlet's Mill* by Giorgio de Santillana and Hertha von Dechend (Godine, Boston, 1977). The two scholarly and patient authors seem quite innocently unaware of the active esoteric traditions and teachings concerning creation of the worlds, the cube and sphere of space, and other such matters which have been taught in magical schools for many centuries. Yet they have proposed that all mythology is derived from a stellar source, and have developed a model very similar to that taught to magical initiates (possibly for millennia), in which the Three Worlds are related to three levels of a Sphere of Space. Our quotation from the Hebrew *Sepher Yetzirah* on page 76 is one of the most widely used examples of this type of teaching, while a classical version is found in the Myth of Er quoted on page 84.

As this model is both traditional and, in the case of the book *Hamlet's Mill*, has a reasoned modern exposition, we should consider it briefly here. It must be emphasised, though, that an astronomical model for mythic patterns is really not separate in any way from an anthropocentric model, in which mortals stand upon the surface of the planet, and make definitions of the sky above, the land at their feet, and the underworld below. The master map or key to both is, of course, the Three Worlds.

We might make a further psychological model, as is done in magical arts, and define the three levels as levels of energy in consciousness, with everyday awareness on the middle, higher or stellar consciousness above, and unconsciousness, or rather *underworld* consciousness, below. There is no conflict between the three models, indeed, they are part of one another and need not be separated falsely.

In an astronomical model of myth, the 'earth' is not literally our planet, but an ideal plane defined through the ecliptic, or through the celestial equator. This divides the zodiac (in whatever form it was customarily presented) into two parts. The northern part, reaching from the spring to the autumn equinox, was the land above or solid principle, while the southern part, reaching from autumn through winter solstice to spring equinox, was the deep waters below.

The Precession of the Equinoxes, by which the great ages of the world were defined by ancient astronomers, poets and seers, causes the Sun to appear to rise from a position within or behind a specific zodiacal sign for a period of approximately 2500 years. The precession is caused by gravitational attraction of the Sun and Moon upon the Earth, giving the planet's rotation a wobble or tilt of about fifty inches per year. This vibration causes the appearance of a slow retrograde motion of the equinoctial points along the ecliptic caused by the tilting of the Earth's axis. The complete cycle in retrograde of the equinoctial points takes approximately 25,800 years, by which time the entire retrograde rotation of twelve signs has occurred (see Figure 4).

This is the origin of the much praised, little understood nonsense concerning the 'Aquarian Age' that is so grossly commercialised today, though in truth the Sun does not move into Aquarius until the next millennium, and we are still firmly in the Piscean epoch of the 'Piscean Age' – and will remain so until long after the year 2000.

Myth, in this astronomical sense, is connected to the long term observation of the positions of the Sun, Moon, and planets, the stars of the Zodiac, and the ages marked out by the precession of the equinoxes. Creation myth, therefore, deals with a period prior to the First Age, and with re-creation that occurs at each turning of the hinge or change of ages as they move through the twelve signs. Each sign causes a different quality or energy complex to attune to the lives of all entities, including humans, and the planet itself.

Those who wish a more detailed exposition of this theory may find it in 'A guide for the perplexed', which appears as an intermezzo between Chapters IV and V of *Hamlet's Mill* as cited above. The astrological exposition, in terms of modern astrology rather than mythic astronomy, may be found in *Astrology* by Jeff Mayo, published by The English Universities Press, 1964.

CREATION MYTHOLOGY: A GENERAL SUMMARY OF THE PATTERNS

We may now proceed to some examples of creation mythology, ranging from those of the ancient civilisations of both East and West, through to variants found in medieval and Renaissance literature, to modern examples which seem to partake of the same traditions. Before looking at typical examples in brief, it is worth recapitulating the basic patterns that have been discussed in the preceding chapters.

A

1. Creation of All Being or universe

2. Creation of worlds, phases or dimensions, and the planet

3. Creation of land

4. Creation of inhabitants:
   (a) races such as humans and others
   (b) orders of animals, birds, fishes
   (c) plants and growing entities

B

1. Relationship of creation myth to inner awareness:
   (a) The stories are individual/racial/regional models to express deep intuitions concerning reality and its progression from abstraction to concretion.
   (b) This has a direct parallel to individual energies; from the deepest unknown source of spiritual and psychic energies and patterns to the outer expression of the body and its continuum of time/space/events.

2. Relationship of creation myth to scientific models from mechanical to advanced stellar physics.

3. The planetary world as a mirror of the universal world.

4. Creation myth is frequently balanced by dissolution myth and apocalyptic vision.

STORY-TELLING

A worldwide story cycle exists which incorporates and was originally generated from mythic perceptions of creation:

1. The origins of All Being
2. The creation of the worlds and their inhabitants
3. The story of the divinities and entities
4. The story of the first and last human, including all ancestral phases or 'histories' stretching from first to last.

In the deepest sense all mythic histories are part of the great story leading from creation to dissolution. For initial purposes of examination and discussion we may make a (false) distinction between those primal myths of creation/dissolution, and the subsequent myths which incorporate social history, cultural phases, and so forth. Thus the creation described in the Old Testament is a true creation myth taken from Hebrew culture and freely altered and translated as an orthodox religious Christian myth. The remainder of the Old Testament, however, with the exception of certain important visions from prophets and specific ancient poems, is not part of the original creation myth, though it does form part of a sequence from creation to dissolution. The dissolving vision is found at the close of the New Testament, with the Apocalypse.

A similar balanced pattern, extending from first to last, is found in many world religions and mythologies. The pagan *Prophecies* and *Life of Merlin* form one British (Welsh or Scots) creation narrative: the *Book of Invasions* is the Irish counterpart. The great Norse and Scandinavian mythic cycles, the Finnish *Kalevala*, and the *Mahabarata* of India are other typical examples. Let us now proceed to some typical creation myths.

PART TWO

CREATION MYTHS AND MEDITATION

5. ANCIENT GREECE

At the deepest or earliest levels of Greek mythology, we find the primordial figure of the Great Mother, deriving historically from Aegean and Cretan civilisation, but actually common to early religion in general. Her role was universal, in the sense that she regulated both the passage of the stars in the heavens and of life, death and rebirth upon earth. Although we make such distinction easily today, it seems likely that the early Aegean concept of the great goddess ruling both the realms above and below made no such division, and that the lower world and the upper were in fact inseparable aspects of one another.

With this great goddess was a male partner, who seems to have been of lesser significance. In ancient Crete the goddess was called Rhea, and was said by the Greeks to have been the mother of Zeus, the ruling god of the classical pantheon. In Aegean mythology the partner to the great goddess was sometimes known as Asterius, which simply means 'starry', and he appears in legend as King Asterion of Crete, who wedded Europa, and was eventually assimilated into the figure of the god Zeus. These connectives merely reflect the passage of a primal goddess and god, connected to earth and stars, into the later pantheon of the Greeks.

One of the major sources for creation mythology in classical Greek tradition is the *Theogony* of Hesiod, written in approximately the eighth century BC. Hesiod was said to have been a contemporary of Homer, and to have bested him in a poetic contest, but much of his biography is legendary rather than historical, and although he himself implies that he lived shortly after the Trojan war, scholars suggest that he actually comes from a later century.

The *Theogony* recounts the origins of the gods and goddesses, their mythic adventures and relationships, and, inevitably, the cosmology associated with such tales. Hesiod's lengthy work is in fact a collection of various traditions in varied styles, often with the same myth being repeated in a number of different versions. 'Theogony' is a term used generally for the history and genealogy of gods, and that set out by Hesiod reflects the traditions of his day. Other more specialised theogonies were found within the Mysteries, perhaps the most famous being that of the Orphic Mystery. The Mysteries employed very specific myths related to traditions of inner transformation and initiation, which were not necessarily part of general or popular tradition. It is from Hesiod that we have our most detailed knowledge of Greek creation mythology, and many of the terms, characters and events that he recounts have passed into literature and general usage, though some have become altered from their original meaning en route.

THE ORIGINATION OF THE GREAT WORLD OR UNIVERSE

Chaos is a word in general use today to mean something prolific, messy, primal, and disorganised, even with negative undertones of destruction or malice. In the *Theogony*, however, the name is used in its proper sense, for Chaos, immense and shadowy, was present in the Beginning. Out of Chaos appeared Gaea, the full breasted Earth, and Eros, the fruitful or attracting force that caused the generation of all beings.

Although it is easy to see this myth as a description of the appearance of the planet Earth, as Gaea, and the procreative force of nature as Eros, it clearly refers to a universal or stellar 'earth' and 'love' of which our natural planet and energies are harmonies or reflections.

The word 'chaos' is derived from a Greek root meaning 'to gape', and represents the quality of space or eternal openness and emptiness. It was originally a cosmic principle, without divine characteristics or attributes; the later definition of chaos as the outpouring of disorganised or 'chaotic' energy and matter in space arose through a mistaken derivation from the root word 'to pour'. Thus we have two distinct meanings to chaos, the pure original cosmic principle of 'gaping' or openness as used by Hesiod, and the later derivation of confused energies and forms prior to ordered manifestation, such entities filling or flowing through the primal space and being ordered by deities. To this is added the corollary that ordered patterns revert to primal chaos at the end of a cycle: this further concept is not in conflict with the original meaning of chaos as openness or emptiness, the void to which all forms and forces return.

Eros, likewise, has a primal and a secondary or derivative definition. In his pure form, as stated by Hesiod, Eros is the universal force of attraction; in later myths he is the god of love, and in even later legends becomes somewhat trivialised as the little godling who causes romantic love, or the sentimental Cupid known in modern popular legend. The universal or cosmic Eros, however, is a power that commands and impels even the gods, and from the power of Eros all energies and events derive.

The *Theogony*, therefore, initially relates a threefold creation myth; from primal Chaos, Gaea, the Great Goddess, arose, a universal world or entity within herself, of which our planet is a direct reflection or lesser form. The next primal force was Eros 'the fire (love) which melts (inflames) hearts', the principle of attraction and cohesion, from whose effect all other entities from stars to stones are born. From this triplication all other forces and forms were created through interaction or reflection, usually represented as generation or copulation.

Chaos also gave birth to Night and Erebus, the powers of darkness; they in turn combined to create Ether and Hemera, the powers of Light or Day. Gaea was mother to Uranus, 'whom she made her equal in grandeur, so that he entirely covered her'. Uranus was visible as the great crown of stars in the night sky, the Zodiac. Thus an active male seeding power is born of a primal female power; the stars are born within the mother womb of space and time.

Gaea next created the high mountains and the still sea of Pontus; this second level or harmonic of creation is a variant of the first level of creation; the high mountains and the still sea, before life forms, are images of primal energies and patterns of differentiation; above and below.

Uranus and Gaea are the great goddess and god of the ancient world, the Sky Father and Earth Mother. They are found in various forms worldwide, and as primordial deities are known in all Indo-European mythology, from Western Europe through Asia to India, where in the Rig-Veda the earth and sky are known as the grandparents of the world. In Greek myth, Uranus remains as a rather undefined figure, and seems to have had no widespread cult or worship in his own right.

Gaea, however, was the Great Mother, the foundation of Greek religion. In a Homeric hymn she is described as 'Gaea, universal mother, firmly founded, oldest of divinities'. Even the gods swore by her, and in Homer's *Iliad*, Hera, the main goddess of the Greek pantheon, rebuts accusations from her partner Zeus by saying 'I swear by Gaea and the vast sky (Uranus) above her'. Thus Gaea underpinned even the gods and goddesses who were ultimately derived from her. She created the universe, the first gods, and even the human race. She was, therefore, connected intimately to the powers of prophecy, and the great oracle of Delphi was originally dedicated to Gaea, before it became the oracle of Apollo. Her image was of the most ancient sort, known even in prehistoric statuettes, the form of a gigantic woman.

The union of Gaea and Uranus, the cosmic mother and father, gave rise to the powerful Titans. These twelve deities, six male and six female, are the elder gods and goddesses of Greek myth, intimately involved with the processes of creation and destruction. In many legends the Titans are at war with the Olympians, and such conflict is often found in world mythology, where various orders of divinities or supernatural beings replace one another as the universe increasingly manifests. Although this sequence of replacement of orders or pantheons is given a historical sociopolitical emphasis in many interpretations of mythology, it equally represents a metaphysical cosmological pattern.

In ancient Greece the Titans were honoured as the original ancestors of humanity; this image of the primal ancestors, semi-human, or proto-human, lies at the roots of many myths and religious traditions. The Titans were the inventors of magic and of the arts . . . which were not, of course, separate originally.

The male Titans were Cronos, Oceanus, Hyperion, Coeus, Crius, and Iapetus; the females Rhea, Mnemosyne, Tethys, Themis, Theia and Phoebe. Rhea, as we have noted above, was the name for the Great Goddess in Cretan mythology, and her appearance as a Titan reflects the constant absorbing and regeneration process that occurs in mythography, when writers attempt to formalise oral traditions and fix them into a specific order within one text. Such a fixing process, of course, is alien to the true nature of mythology, which was originally oral, protean, and quite deliberately amorphous in many ways. The mythic process is one of perpetual re-creation, so the rigid boundaries and pantheons of state religion or intellectual analysis are always broken down or undermined by the true force of myth itself.

Uranus and Gaea next bred the Cyclopes, the famous one-eyed entities, who are chthonic or primal underworld forces, as are the Titans. In Hesiod's poem they are

Figure 4 The Wheel of the Zodiac

The Twelve Signs of the Zodiac are a familiar sight today in popular publications, wall charts, and personal jewellery. But this trivial level of astrology masks a number of deeper and older phases of the art. Modern astrology, based upon mathematical or idealised calculation rather than observation, has repeatedly proven its worth, though it is still the subject of much debate. Earlier forms of astrology, however, depended extensively upon observation, or upon a fusion of observation and patterns of calculation. The earliest astrology was mythic astronomy, and the Twelve Signs are mythic potencies or entities deriving from combination of the Four Elements of Air, Fire, Water and Earth.

The creatures or symbols of the Zodiac are in themselves a creation tale or cycle, and many mythic themes are related to them. The Precession of the Equinoxes (see page 36–8) generates a major stream of mythology worldwide, due to long term observation of sidereal patterns.

Many myths and legends employ personae or deities who are identical or closely related to the signs of the Zodiac. The Zodiac used extensively in the Western world is derived from a fusion of Arabic, Babylonian, and Greek sources; but the underlying unity of zodiacal emblems suggests that they are not merely traditional images, or a matter of observation and calculation, but an inherent property of imagination and consciousness.

Many of the implications and uses of the zodiacal and elemental systems and world-views have been lost to the modern world, but one that is worth special mention is that of the *Art of Memory* in which the sphere of the Zodiac was visualised and items of note or knowledge located in each *decanate* or sector. This not only generated in turn a detailed system of information storage, but would give symbolic answers to specified problems through interaction between the various items employed and the Signs or sub-symbols of the decanates themselves.

In meditational or visualising arts, the creatures or emblems of the Zodiac are brought to life in a simpler manner, through building their images as strongly as possible and attuning to the energies which they embody. This in turn is closely related to the primal or shamanistic and magical art of working with totem animals, many of which are also found as Elemental Beasts or Zodiacal Signs.

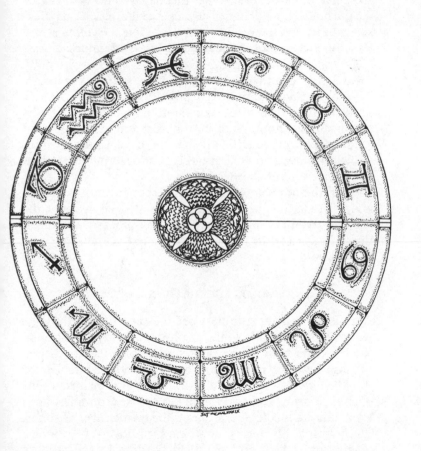

49

associated with storms or elemental forces: Brontes or thunder, Steropes, lightning; Arges, the thunderbolt. The last offspring were the Hecatoncheires or Hundred Handed Ones. Of these there were but three, Gyges, Cottus, and Briareus, each with a hundred arms and fifty heads attached to their backs. Gyges means large-limbed, Cottus means furious, while Briareus means vigorous. Thus there is a general connection between the Titans, Cyclopes, and Hecatoncheires and the elemental forces of nature.

As each of these successive orders or types of deity were born, Uranus shut them deep within the earth. Eventually Gaea planned to destroy her first mate, Uranus, in retribution for his imprisonment of their offspring. She produced gleaming metal from her bosom, and fashioned a sickle or *harpe* from it. Only her last born, Cronos, would strike the blow, and as Uranus slept he castrated his father, and cast the genitals into the sea.

From this terrible wound blood seeped into the earth, giving rise to the Furies, to giants, and to tree nymphs, the ash tree dwellers or Meliae. From the pieces that floated upon the sea a white foam was generated, which gave form to Aphrodite, goddess of love.

THE COSMOLOGY OF THE ORPHIC MYSTERIES

At this point in our summary of Greek creation mythology, we may return briefly to the Orphic cosmology mentioned earlier. This is a more refined metaphysical tradition, having a practical or initiatory aspect, in which members of the Mystery cult ritualised or underwent transformations of consciousness related to the Orphic tradition. Orpheus was a divine musician and poet, the great singer of songs. The Orphic Mysteries combined philosophy, science, magic, mysticism, and practical training in the esoteric arts. The myth of Orpheus seeking to rescue Eurydice from the Underworld is one of the most compelling and enduring mythic tales known to humanity.

The Orphic tradition, partly refined and stated by the priest Onomacritus, makes a number of detailed changes to the popular creation cycle stated in Hesiod. Time, or Cronos, was said to be the first principle out of which then arose Chaos, the infinite, and Ether, the finite. Chaos was enveloped by Night, and within this envelope the creative Ether generated cosmic material. The entire organisation became a type of egg, with Night as the surrounding shell. The upper part of the Orphic egg was the vault of the heavens, while the lower part was the earth. In the centre of this egg was the first being, Phanes, the Light. Light conjoined with Night or darkness, and so created the material Heaven and earth. Phanes was also said to be the originator of Zeus. Let us now move on, and find how the primal creation is represented in Scandinavian mytholology.

6.

SCANDINAVIA AND ICELAND

The major sources for Scandinavian, and indeed Teutonic, mythology are the *Eddas*. These collections of poems and prose, many of which predate the advent of Christianity, were originally the oral sources of knowledge, history, poetry, cosmology and mythology. They were written out and preserved by medieval authors, often remaining anonymous, from Iceland, Norway, Sweden and Denmark. These sources, deriving, as is always the case with mythology, from an extensive and complex oral tradition, reveal the beliefs concerning the creation of the worlds that were prevalent until at least as late as the thirteenth century in Scandinavia. By this period the countries concerned were officially Christian, but as in Ireland, where pagan sagas seeming to date from the Bronze Age were preserved by ninth-century monastic scribes, Scandinavian chroniclers of Christian profession preserved the bardic or skaldic lore of earlier centuries. We shall find that they have much in common with the other mythic traditions of creation.

The Scandinavian myths preserved in the *Eddas* are not necessarily complete, and in some texts alternative forms of the same myth or legend are happily juxtaposed or combined. We find this organic and (apparently) indiscriminate growth of tales in other early collections, such as Hesiod's *Theogony*, the Homeric epics, the early Irish sagas, and indeed most early texts dealing with cosmogony, mythology, religion, and legend. Even official dogmatic religious texts, still in use today, are full of what appear to be illogical contradictions. Completeness and logical sequences, however, are of far less value than gaining insights and appreciation of the major themes and models in any mythic collections.

In Icelandic sources, which preserved much pagan lore until a surprisingly late period, we find a creation myth similar in some ways to that of Ancient Greece, yet stamped with the unique characteristic of the icy north. Similarities between traditions do not necessarily imply borrowing or copying, and it is altogether too simplistic to assume that any one source, theme, or image, is directly borrowed from another, even if there is a period of time and cultural exchange between them which might suggest such transmission. Oral traditions are essentially timeless, and do not always correspond or attune to historical periods and events in the way that one might assume. This is particularly true when we talk of the deepest strata of myth in which primal forces of creation and the oldest gods are described.

First, according to the poets of Iceland, there was an abyss which stretched unceasingly through space. This abyss, or void, called Ginnungagap in the *Eddas*, is a concept of pre-creation that appears in all mythic mystical, magical and religious traditions, though often it is lost underneath later accretions of increasingly politicised myth and legend. Co-existent with the abyss is often the concept of a pre-primal deity or all pervading entity: to the Norse this concept was sometimes identified with the All-father.

Figure 5 The Tree of Life

The *Tree of Life* is found worldwide. The most abstract yet comprehensive variant is the Kabbalistic Tree, shown here, based upon Jewish oral mystical tradition; its origins are unknown. It is probably a fusion of the naturalistic tree emblem sacred to ancient European cultures, with concepts of dimensions, spheres or modes of creation preserved in ancient Greek, Eastern, and near-Eastern metaphysics. Whatever its origins, it makes a comprehensive map for creation mythology, cosmology, religion, and meditation or magical arts.

The *Tree of Life* has undergone many developments in literature from the medieval period to the present day, often losing its exclusively Hebraic attributes such as sacred letters and angelic and divine Names, becoming increasingly connected to world mythology. Pan-cultural flexibility is the great feature of the Tree, for, providing its proper structure and relative units are understood, it may be employed within a fusion of differing symbolic systems.

The basics of the Tree, rendered into a simple list of correspondences, are as follows:

The First Triad

1. **The Crown**: Original Being emanates from the Void. Traditionally associated with the First Breath or Holy Spirit.

2. **Wisdom**: The utterance of stars within space: Spiralling Nebulae, the Zodiac, the Star-Father.

3. **Understanding**: The womb of time and space; the Great Mother. Traditionally associated with the planet Saturn.

The *Abyss* or Chaotic Void: Supernal or Divine Being rises above the Void as the First Triad; the Second Triad (4, 5, 6) is reflected below the Void, reaching towards material manifestation and organic life. The Third Triad (7, 8, 9) is a reflection of the Second, each reflection being a lower harmonic and inversion of that above. (see the *Sepher Yetzirah*, page 75)

The Second Triad

4. **Mercy**: The anabolic surge of forces towards form. Traditionally associated with Jupiter and related generous outpouring powerful divinities.

5. **Severity**: Negative or purifying power; catabolic breakdown of patterns. Traditionally associated with Mars, and in many mythic traditions with a goddess of death, or destruction. Examples include the Irish *Morrigan* or Phantom Queen, Hindu *Kali* and the *Black Isis* of ancient Egypt.

6. **Beauty**: Harmonising central Sun, source of Light. This Sphere unifies powers of Giving and Taking into Balance: all Saviours, Redeemers, Sons of Light and solar gods and goddesses are associated here.

The Third Triad

7. **Victory**: The Sphere of Venus, forces of attraction, emotion, polarising energies of life. Goddesses of Dawn and Evening, of Love, of enlightenment through devotion.

8. **Honour/Glory**: The Sphere of Mercury, associated with mental agility, analytical energy, increasing development of creative force towards interactive form. Also with messenger gods mediating between humanity and the solar deity.

9. **Foundation**: The Sphere of the Moon: all lunar gods and goddesses, powers of fertility, regeneration, birth and physical death. The sphere of dreams and intimations, of secret matrices behind physical form.

10. **Kingdom**: The outer or manifest worlds, Planet Earth. This ultimate Sphere embodies all the previous Nine. Goddesses of the Land, the Earth Mother, and orders of humanity, animals, and plants inhabit this Sphere. The Four Elements manifest as Four Planetary Directions, Four Winds, and Four Seasons.

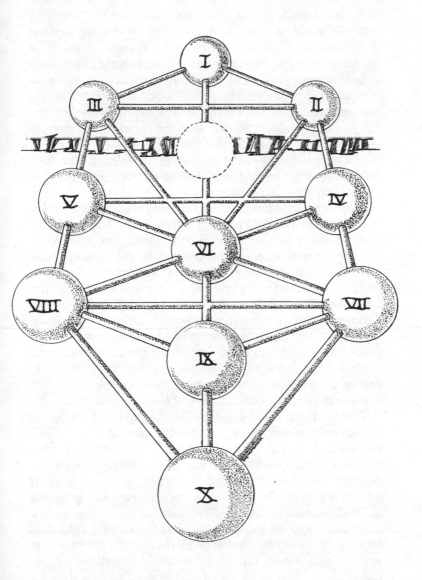

The first world or zone to form out of the abyss was Niflheim, consisting of shadows and clouds. Niflheim defined the region to the north of the void: and this pattern of definition, with the first zones, beings or energies defining the directions, dimensions and worlds that were to follow, occupies much of the awareness and tradition of creation mythology. The four directions of north, south, east and west, play important roles in creation mythology, not in any ignorant sense in which primitive people assumed that other worlds were literally to the north but as cosmological or cosmographical realities. The four directions of the human world were mirrors or harmonics of the Four Powers or Directions of the Universe.

In the most sophisticated variants of creation mythology, the entire model is spherical: this gives rise to basic directions of Above, Below, North, South, East and West; and these in turn are often related to the concept of a human figure standing upon the line of the horizon, with other directions relative to the orientation of the body. In more subtle metaphysical models, such as the Platonic solids, the basic concept of the upright human within a sphere or field of orientated energy or awareness gives rise to mathematical models of the universe. Such models are still being developed by modern physicists, and in a paradoxical sense, these are the direct heirs of the world-views or cosmologies of the ancients.

The northern world of Niflheim held the fountain Hvergelmir which gave out twelve glacial rivers, and was indeed the source of all rivers. The northern quarter of Niflheim (the north of the north) was filled with frozen glaciers and ice-mountains from Elivagar (Icy Waves) which had been present there forever. Poison encrusted the frozen scum of ice from Elivagar.

To the south of the void or abyss another world was originated, being the balance to that of the north. This was Muspellsheim, the realm of fire. Muspellsheim was the abode of Surt the Fire-Giant, who wielded a flaming sword: his presence was at the beginning and the ending of creation, for at Ragnarök, the apocalypse of Norse myth, he was to fling fire over all things. When the hot rivers of the south touched the icy rivers of the north, the solidifying bitter principle became coated with thick frost, which partially filled the abyss between the two extremes.

The hoar frost within the abyss was in turn softened by warm winds from the south, and from its melting droplets the body of Ymir or Aurgelmir (Mud-Seether) was formed, a giant with a form similar to that of a human, the first living being. From Ymir came the race of Frost Giants, the first male and female of which were generated from the sweat of his left armpit. More specifically, Ymir became profusely bathed in sweat while sleeping, and the first pair of giants were formed under his left arm. One of his feet generated a son upon the other.

The melting ice also generated a cow, who became the wet-nurse of the giants, known as Audumla. From her udders flowed four streams of milk, from which Ymir drank. Audumla licked the blocks of primal ice, and was sustained by the salt contained within them. Through her licking she gradually liberated, from the hair of the head downwards, through the passage of three days, the body of a new type of being, Buri, whose son Bor coupled with the giant daughter Bestla (daughter of Bölthorn or Evil-Thorn) to create the gods Odin, Vili, and Vé.

This new order of beings immediately began to destroy the primal giants, beginning with their progenitor Ymir.

The copious blood of Ymir filled the abyss between the worlds of north and south, Niflheim and Muspellsheim, and drowned the Giants. But one Giant, Bergelmir, escaped with his mate in a small boat, and from them a new race of giants arose.

The sons of Bor, however, raised the corpse of Ymir, and made of it Midgard or the middle world, halfway between the two primal zones of ice and fire. From Ymir's flesh the land was made, and from his blood the great sea. From his hair trees were fashioned, and from his bones the high mountains. The skull of Ymir was raised high upon four immense pillars (defining the Four Directions) and so formed the vault of the heavens. Within this vault the sparks of energy from Muspellsheim formed the stars, sun and moon. The passage of the stars and planets was ruled by the gods, and the passing of the sun across the sky generated the first blades of grass upon the earth below. The brains of Ymir were thrown into the winds, and so made the clouds.

The sons of Bor were joined by other gods, and working with Odin they constructed Asgard, the great hall of the gods, where each deity had his or her own palace. Between Asgard and Midgard was built the rainbow bridge, Bifrost.

But the corpse of Ymir was still to generate further life; from maggots within it the dwarves were born, living within the earth from which they were formed, and endowed with human-like form and intelligence.

Humanity, however, was formed from two trees, *Ask* (ash) and *Embla* (vine), by three of the gods. Odin gave them breath, Hoenir gave them souls and reasoning abilities, and Lodur gave them the warmth and colour of life itself. From these two primal people, formed of trees by the gods, came the race of humankind.

THE THREE WORLDS AND WORLD TREE

Norse mythology includes the widespread image or cosmology of Three Worlds, set in a specific relationship to one another. The exact relationship of the worlds varies, but the general pattern is that Midgard, the middle or planetary world of Earth and humanity, was surrounded by a vast ocean, in which dwelt the all-encircling Midgard serpent. Below Midgard was Niflheim, the Mist World, land of the dead. This Underworld was ruled by the goddess Hel, and its gateway was guarded against the living by the terrible hound Garm. Above the middle world was the world of the gods.

The triple creation pattern, found in other Indo-European mythologies, seems to be a further development upon the primal creation myth described above, though it is considerably clarified by visualising a triple spiral, with the worlds interpenetrating one another, rather than hard and fast divisions.

The unifying emblem in Norse or Teutonic mythology is the tree Yggdrasil (see Figure 6). From the primal creation mythology of realms emerging from the abyss or void, a vision of three worlds was gradually developed. Yggdrasil grew through each of the Three Worlds, and may be represented in a number of different ways, depending upon our interpretation of the model as spherical, spiral, circular, or as a two dimensional map of three rings or adjoining superimposed worlds. Perhaps the simplest summary would be to visualise the tree as a real but paradoxical tree, growing through all possible worlds. This is certainly the attitude taken by the early poets who recounted the tales of the gods and goddesses, of creation and destruction.

Yggdrasil was an evergreen ash tree; its central root penetrated deep into the Underworld, while its crown reached to the uppermost levels of the overworld or universal sky. The early *skalds* also knew the tree as The Steed of the Redoubtable or of Odin; this was often rationalised as meaning that Odin's divine horse drew sustenance from the leaves of Yggdrasil, but it also has the underlying meaning that the tree was a vehicle, a source of power and movement, through the worlds.

Beside the root that tapped into Niflheim or Nifhel rose the primal fountain Hvergelmir, source of the great rivers. A second root tapped into the icy realm of the Giants, within which was the fountain Mimir, source of all wisdom. So great was the potency of this fountain that Odin was willing to lose one eye to drink of it. The third root of the tree, which in certain traditions seems to paradoxically reach into the stars, revealed the fountain of Urd, greatest of the Norns or Fates. The water of this fountain or well was drawn every day by the Norns, who sprinkled the foliage and branches of Yggdrasil to keep them alive and flourishing. The concept of a root penetrating deep and finally emerging into the deepest sky, the region of the stars, is an important image found

Figure 6 Yggdrasil, the World Ash

Yggdrasil, the World Tree of Norse mythology, is a fusion of a naturalistic image with a metaphysical model of the created worlds. In its simplest sense it is a variant of *The Three Worlds* (see Figure 1), but like all mythic images it has a unique quality deriving from its region and its people. Because tree images are frequently employed by primal cultures, it is often assumed that they are merely crude ways of interpreting the world or of simplifying mysterious creation processes, likening the universe to a great tree, This is far from the case. The descriptions of gods, men, animals, birds, and mythic beasts that inhabit the Tree and the Three Worlds through which it grows (see page 63) are, in their own way, a complex sophisticated and remarkably coherent and subtle vision of creation.

It is clear that such descriptions and images were not meant to remain upon a superficial literal or superstitious level, for they hold a wealth of information about the forces and forms of the created worlds, and about the polarities of creation and destruction; once the language of the imagery is grasped, it becomes coherent and comprehensible. This symbolic language, like that of many ancient myths, is one of nature, of the elements, of orders or categories of beings, and of specific animals in roles connected to powers, and the forces of life and death.

Yggdrasil is the product of a long oral tradition, but refined and formalised by the work of professional poets; originally it would have been a major emblem for the pagan religion of Northern Europe, linked in many ways to the tree cults of the ancient Celts and to the simpler religious concepts of the later Saxons, who worshipped a world tree, known as the *Irminsul*.

Yggdrasil is a complex and in many ways paradoxbzical emblem: initially it represents three worlds, that of the gods above, humanity in the middle, and the terrible underworld forces below. But we also find that it has one of its roots in the realm of the gods so it was not always regarded as a 'linear' growth from Below to Above. A similar paradox is found in the Kabbalistic Tree of Life, upon which the material world or *Kingdom* is said to be identical to the highest spiritual source, the *Crown*.

It seems likely that the original Norse creation myth described the appearance of three worlds out of primal Ice and Fire (see page 53) and that the refinement of the World Tree is a later development, but it is nevertheless of ancient origin and tradition, and like many such world trees formed an integral part of the religion, myth and culture of its people.

in many chthonic or Underworld myths. It reveals an intuition that the universe is inherent in the depths of the earth, that spirit is present in matter. In modern physics we find this ancient metaphysical theory curiously supported by theories of atomic and sub-atomic forces, waves and particles.

In the upper branches of the Tree a golden cock stood watch, ready to give warning of attack by the Giants who were sworn to destroy the *Aesir* or gods. Beneath the tree was buried the magical horn of Heimdall, which was fated to sound the call to the last battle between the gods and the forces of destruction. The Aesir met in a sacred spot by the trunk of the tree, where the goat Heidrun grazed and gave nourishing milk to the warriors of Odin.

Thus a further triple division or harmonic (Above, Below, Middle or Within) was seen in connection with the tree that grew through the Three Worlds, which themselves were generally conceived of as Above, Below, and Middle.

Below the third root of the tree was the giant serpent Nidhögg which gnawed ceaselessly at the root, seeking to bring the tree down. Through the great branches four stags roamed, devouring the buds and young leaves. These negative forces counterbalanced the positive forces of the Norns, who nourished the tree. This image embodied the balance between the forces of creation and destruction within the all-prevalent tree, just as these same forces upon a universal level were represented by ice and fire in the primal creation myth.

The tree was not only a cosmological model, but was used as a focus for religious devotions in daily life. Tree worship was a fusion of very simple or primal magic, in which spirits or ancestors were regarded as dwelling within the tree, to sophisticated religious philosophy, in which the growing trees, or in some cases artificial pillars, were seen as emblems of the Great Tree. In the eighth century the conquering Charlemagne destroyed a sacred tree-pillar, Irminsul, in Westphalia, thus seeking to subjugate the Saxons by wiping out their focus of worship and identity.

The Icelandic *Prose Edda* of Snorri Sturluson (written around AD 1200) describes Yggdrasil as follows:

That ash is of all trees the most huge and stately. Its branches overhang all worlds and strike out above the heavens. The three roots of the tree, spreading far and wide, support it aloft: one root is with the gods, another with the Frost Giants, where formerly there used to be the yawning abyss, and the third stands over Niflheim. Under that root is the Roaring Cauldron called Hvergelmir with the dragon Nidhögg gnawing at the root from below. Under the root which twists towards the Frost Giants there is the well of Mimir, for Mimir is the name of the well-warden. Mimir is filled with wisdom for he drinks from the well out of the Giallarhorn ... The third root of the ash stands in heaven; beneath it is the spring, exceedingly sacred, the well of Urdr. There the gods have their judgement seat. Every day, over the rainbow bridge Bifröst, the Powers ride to it; that is why it is called the bridge of the Aesir ... An eagle roosts in the boughs of the ash tree, wise beyond all knowing, and between his eyes sits the hawk Vedrfolnir. A squirrel, named Ratatosk darts up and down the tree bearing spiteful tales between the eagle and Nidhögg. Four stags browse over the branches of the ash and nibble at the bark. I will tell you their names: Dainn, Dvalinn, Duneyrr, Durathrorr. And with Nidhögg in Hvergelmir there is such a nest of serpents that no tongue can possibly tell of them ... It is said that the Norns dwelling around the well of Urdr take water every day and mix it with gravel lying about the well and sprinkle it over the ash to prevent its branches from withering or rotting. The dew which drips to the ground beneath the tree is called honeydew by men, and bees are nourished upon it. The well of Urdr gives life to two birds named Swans, from whom are descended all birds of that kind so called.

The divine bird leads us to a number of mythologies, including Celtic, Amerindian, Greek, and our next example, that of Finland.

7. FINLAND

The source for Finnish mythology is a vast collection of popular songs, narratives, and epic fragments. These were assembled into one unit in the nineteenth century, and various collectors and scholars have worked with the material since, expanding the collection considerably. The Finnish tales are particularly important as they constitute a living tradition of myth-singing that perpetuated into modern historical times.

In the Finnish *Kalevala*[16], we find the following creation myth:

Ilma, goddess of the air, had a daughter, Luonnotar. Luonnotar dwelt alone in the stars, but growing tired of her single virgin state, allowed herself to fall into the great sea below, and to float upon the wave-crests. Rocked to and fro, the breath of the wind caressed her, and the power of the sea made her fertile. She floated upon this fertilising sea for seven hundred years, and could find no resting place.

At length she met a duck (or, in some variants, an eagle) who flew across the sea seeking a nesting place. The duck saw Luonnotar's knee, and here he built his nest. (Note that the bird is male.) When he had laid his eggs, and sat for three days upon them, they became fertile.

Then did the daughter of Ilma feel scorching heat upon her skin; she bent her knee violently and the eggs rolled into the deep. They were not lost in the slime below, but were changed into beautiful and excellent things. From the lower part of the eggs the earth was formed, mother of all living creatures. From their upper part the sublime heavens were formed. The egg yolk became the radiant yellow sun, and the white the gleaming moon. The spotted fragment became the stars, and the black fragments the clouds in the air.

Luonnotar then began the work of shaping creation: islands emerged from the waters, promontories were raised, gulfs created and shorelines laid out . . .

The concept of the worlds forming out of fragments of a primal order or life-form pervades creation mythology. We find it again in the myths of ancient Babylon.

8. ANCIENT BABYLON

The creation myths usually referred to as Babylonian originate from a period long before the great civilisations of Assur or Babylon which developed and perpetuated them. In an archaeological or historical sense, these are among the oldest written records of creation myths known in the world, but we should not assume that they are necessarily originals or sources for myths that were recorded at a historical later date. Nevertheless, Assyrio-Babylonian myths help us to realise that the main themes found in creation mythology date back many thousands of years in certain cultures or civilisations. In brief, the origins of these myths date back at least as far as the Sumerian and Akkadian civilisations which grew upon the fertile lower banks of the rivers Tigris and Euphrates, as early as three thousand years BC, and possibly from an even earlier period of time.

The creation myth of the Babylonians, who developed out of the Sumerians and Akkadians into one of the greatest civilisations known, are preserved upon seven inscribed tablets. These along with other texts were excavated from the library of Ashurbanipal, in Nineveh. The tablets date to around 1000 BC, and are likely to be based upon older sources, possibly older inscriptions or oral tradition.

THE CREATION FROM THE WATERS

Two watery primal elements or principles are described in Babylonian creation myth: Tiamat, or salty and bitter water, and Apsu, or sweet water. From the commingling of these two primal polarised sources, arose Mummu the tumultuous waves, from which came the creation of other beings.

Apsu was, more specifically, a watery abyss surrounding the primal earth, which is described as a disc with high mountains at its perimeter. The mountains supported the heavens, and were in turn supported upon the waters of Apsu. All springs which reached the surface of the earth came from Apsu, which had a connotation of a male principle. But at this earliest stage the abyss filled with Apsu held no earth.

Tiamat was a female principle, and was embodied within the primal seas, which were salty. She was understood as a chaotic procreative power, often hostile to the organising functions of the later gods and goddesses. The concept of Mummu the tumultuous waves, is the result of the interaction of the two polarised forces: this is not dissimilar to certain theories of modern physics, in which waves or resonances of energy interact to form the universe.

As the mythology moves from primal forces towards increasingly detailed entities, we find the birth of two serpents, Lakhmu and Lakhamu, who in turn generated Anshar and Kishar. These two were male and female powers, who represented the primal first celestial and terrestrial or upper and lower worlds, earlier forms of the starry sky and the earth of the created planet. From Anshar and Kishar were born two orders of spiritual being, the Igigi or sky gods, and the Anunnaki or underworld gods, who also inhabited the earth. Thus the polarised pattern, which began in the cosmic abyss with the waters of Apsu and Tiamat, was reflected right through into the division, or rather complementary polarisation, of the gods of over-earth and under-earth.

The newly created gods were so energetic that they disturbed the primordial rest of Apsu, who planned with Tiamat to destroy them. The great god Ea, however, became aware of this plan, through his perception of all that came to pass. Through powerful magic he entrapped both Apsu and Mummu, thus earning the hatred of Tiamat. The further development of the myths involves the increasing conflict between the orders of deities, with Tiamat generating monstrous creatures and rising up to fight the gods of order and pattern.

The climax of this complex conflict was the battle between Bêl-Marduk, who became ruler of the gods, and Tiamat.

Bêl-Marduk is one of the earliest forms of a great solar deity ... his image percolated through history and may be found within those of St Michael and St George in Christian mythology thousands of years separated from Babylon. The bright hero who slays a dragon is part of the solar phase of creation myth or cosmology. Once Marduk had slain Tiamat, she was dismembered to form the constituents of a new world order, which included the creation of humanity.

Marduk's weapons were elemental, a storm chariot, a hurricane, lightning, and bow, arrows, and net. The *Epic of Creation* describes how Marduk caught Tiamat in his net, and loosed the terrible hurricane into her face:

> She opened her mouth, Tiamat, to swallow him,
> He drove in the hurricane so that she could not close her lips.
> The terrible wind filled her belly.
> Her heart was seized,
> She held her mouth agape.
> He let fly his arrow, and pierced her belly.
> Her bowels he clove, her heart he split.
> He made her powerless, destroyed her life.

He felled her body and stood triumphant on it.

(From *The Epic of Creation*, Tablet IV, verses 96–104.
Adapted from various translations.)

The dismemberment of Tiamat, like that of Ymir in Norse creation myth, enabled the construction of a new world. One half of her body made the heavens or sky, while the other made the earth. Marduk created human beings to worship the gods and bring joy to their hearts; after humanity the rivers of the world, the plants, and the animals were made. We may note here that creation myths often place the appearance of humanity before that of plants and animals, which is the opposite of the materialist concept of evolution. The esoteric teaching, found in both Eastern and Western spiritual traditions, is that humanity was a very early form of creation, made in the image of divinity, and that humankind in turn went through several phases of increasing devolution to reach their present condition within the physical world. This is reflected in the Biblical myth of the Garden of Eden, in which humanity is created in a model of perfection, but 'falls', or is manifested outwards into an increasingly physical world and body.

Marduk took on characteristics of the primal gods, and to him became attached the powers of his father Ea, and of the primal god Bêl. The root-word Bêl, meaning bright or shining, was a potent god-name for thousands of years, and is found in many contexts and languages where a solar or fiery deity is referred to. Marduk was known as:

The light of the father who begot him,
Renewer of the gods,
Lord of pure incantation, causing the dead to live again,
He who knows the hearts of gods,
Guardian of Justice and of law,
Creator of all things,
Among lords the first,

Ruler of Kings,
Shepherd of Gods.

At this point the creation mythology opens out into the tales of the gods of the seven planets, the Underworld, the heroes, and history of humankind. Although we have typified Marduk as incorporating solar attributes, there was also an important triad of Moon, Sun, and Venus. This triad commences with the Moon god Sîn, who is father to the great goddess Ishtar, or Venus, and to Shamash the Sun. It seems likely that this triad represents a very ancient mythology, into which Marduk was later incorporated. The historical and sociopolitical ramifications of mythology and worship are not, as has been said previously, directly involved in creation myth, being later unfoldments and developments within the mythic timescale. Even when serious political attempts have been made to change creation myth by a powerful religion, as with the Egyptian example of Akhnaton who developed a personal solar cult counter to the flow of the great myths and religions, or with the Judaeo-Christian corruption of the earliest myths of creation, some of the foundation of the original mythology always remains.

We may now briefly compare the Babylon creation myth with that found in Tibetan Buddhism, for both contain the perennial imagery of interleaved worlds and sacred mountains.

9. TIBETAN BUDDHIST COSMOGRAPHY

Tibetan Buddhist cosmography is related to Brahmanic teaching and interpretation, but includes certain unique elements which probably derive from the chthonic magical cult of Tibet prior to the adoption of Buddhism. A description of Tibetan cosmography is given by W. Y. Evans Wentz in *The Tibetan Book Of The Dead* (Oxford University Press, 1985) and the following summary is based in part upon this description.

Both Buddhist and Hindu cosmography revolve, literally, around a sacred mountain, which acts as a pivot for all worlds, all universes. Most widely known as Mount Meru or Ri-rab in Tibetan, it has the same role as the great ash tree Yggdrasil, the Finnish world-oak, or the Tree of Life. Mount Meru is surrounded by seven concentric circles of waters or oceans, separated by seven concentric circles of golden mountains. Beyond the fourteen circles of waters and mountains is the circle of the continents or lands. Thus the universe, or more accurately we should say the 'multi-verse', for it occupies more than the regular spatial dimensions, may be likened to fifteen interleaving circles or spheres, with the sacred mountain rising through them. This definition gives us a typical model of the Sacred Directions: Above, Below, Within, East, South, West and North.

The concept of base and apex is used to define levels or worlds of consciousness and energy; the summit of the sacred mountain supports various levels of paradise, the uppermost of which is the supreme heaven, the penultimate realm of being before the void or Nirvana. This corresponds to the crown of the Tree of Life, the unified primal consciousness or world of spiritual Being. In the nether realms below the mountain, however, are the various hells traditionally found in Buddhism or Hinduism, while between the hells and the highest paradise, are graded degrees or worlds.

Within Mount Meru are four realms or dimensions, one above the other. The uppermost of these is occupied by titanic supernatural beings (Asuras), cast out of the heavens. The three lower realms are occupied by orders of spirits or lesser supernatural beings. This fourfold vertical hierarchy is similar to those found in the angelogy of Judaeo-Christian mysticism and mythology, and compares interestingly with the heretical cosmography described in the medieval *Vita Merlini* (see page 103)

The outermost ring or sphere, the fifteenth, has the primal continents floating upon the outermost ocean. The fifteenfold sphere is enclosed by an iron wall, which is the barrier or threshold between universes, and encloses and reflects the light of sun, moon, and stars. Many universes are postulated. Within each universe, the alternation of subtle fluid (water, the oceans) and material substance (the mountains) creates the resonance of balance and interaction.

In the Tibetan *Bardo Thödol*, or *Book of the Dead*, the outermost ocean supports four continents, each one located at one of the Four Directions. Each continent has a left- and right-hand satellite continent, giving twelve primal continents or directions in all. Thus we have the model of a twelvefold universe, based upon the concepts of height, depth, and the Four Directions. The continents are not literally those of this planet, but are in fact worlds that are both physical and metaphysical. They represent, to a certain extent, planetary entities such as our Earth (the Southern Continent), the Moon (the Eastern Continent), the Sun (the Western Continent), but should not be confused with the literal planets. As in all creation mythology, the directions and worlds represent potentialities as well as actualities: the air, fire, water and earth, elements of creation, lead into many worlds through their inherent resonance, or potentiality as gates or modes of transformative power (see Figures 3 and 7).

Mount Meru itself has Four Faces, each being of a sacred substance and colour; a typical pattern would be: Silver in the East, Jasper in the South, Ruby in the West, and Gold in the North, though traditions may vary.

The complexities and harmonies of interleaved worlds or universes are the main feature of Jewish mysticism and Platonic and Neo-Platonic cosmology. We can now begin to examine typical examples of these major schools or modes of Creation Myth.

10. THE CREATION IN HEBREW MYSTICISM

The *Sepher Yetzirah* is a Jewish cosmological text, attributed to Rabbi Akiba who lived in the early part of the second century AD. As with most cosmological texts rooted in ancient tradition, it seems likely that the writer was not the sole inventor or author; the character of the *Sepher Yetzirah* is such that it combines creation mythology with precise mystical and metaphysical terminology. It is likely, therefore, that it is a development of a myth or sacred text preserved outside orthodoxy by its inherent sanctity. This text and a number of similar books from Hebrew mysticism have had a significant effect upon the development of both Renaissance and modern magical arts, particularly through study and use by nineteenth century magical orders such as the Hermetic Order of the Golden Dawn. Such relatively modern reinterpretations, however, do not alter the kernel of mythic or perennial cosmology.

LINES FROM THE *SEPHER YETZIRAH*

1. In thirty-two wondrous Paths of Wisdom did Yah, Yahveh Tzabaoth, (Lord of Hosts) the Gods of Israel, the Elohim (Living Ones), the King of Ages, the merciful and gracious God, the Exalted One, the Dweller in Eternity, most high and holy – engrave His Name by the three Sepharim (modes of manifestation) – Numbers, Letters, and Sounds.

2. Ten are the (ineffable Sephiroth or Spheres) Voices from the Void. Twenty-two are the Letters, the Foundation of all things; there are Three Mothers, Seven Double, and Twelve Simple Letters.

3. The Voices from the Void are Ten, so are the numbers; and as there are in man five fingers upon five, so over them is established a covenant of strength, by word of mouth, and by circumcision.

4. Ten is the number of the Voices from the Void, ten and not nine, ten and not eleven. Understand this wisdom, and be wise in its perception. Search out concerning it, restore the Word to the Creator, and replace Him who formed it upon his throne.

5. The Ten Voices from the Void have ten vast regions bonded to them; boundless in origin and without end; an abyss of good and evil, measureless height and depth; unbounded to the East and to the West; unbounded to the North and to the South; and the Lord the one God, the Faithful King rules all these from his holy Throne for ever and ever.

6. The Ten Voices from the Void appear as a flash of lightning; their origin is unseen and without end. The Word is in them as they emanate and return, they speak as from the whirlwind and on returning fall prostrate in adoration before the Throne.

7. The Ten Voices from the Void, whose end is in their beginning, arise like fire from burning coal. For God is

superlative in unity, there is no equal to Him; what number may be placed before One?

8. Ten are the Voices from the Void; let your lips be sealed lest you speak of them, let your heart be guarded as you meditate upon them; if your mind runs away bring it back under your control; even as it is said, running and returning, as the living creatures, and so is the Covenant made.

9. The Voices from the Void give out Ten numbers: *First* the Spirit of the Gods of the Living; blessed and more than blessed be the Living God of Ages. The Voice, the Spirit, the Word, these are of the Holy Spirit.

Second from the Spirit He produced Air, and within it shaped twenty-two sounds . . . the letters. Three are Mothers, Seven are Double, and Twelve are Simple, but the Spirit is first above all these.

Third from the Air He shaped the Waters, and from the formless void shaped mud and clay, designed surfaces upon them, and hewed out hollows within them, so forming the powerful material Foundation.

Fourth from the Water he shaped Fire, and made a Throne of Glory with Auphanim (Wheels), Seraphim (Flaming Serpents) and Chioth Ha Qadesh (Holy Living Creatures), as his ministers. And with these three He completed His dwelling, so it is written, 'Who makes His angels spirits and His ministers a flaming fire.'

He chose three from among the simple letters and sealed them, forming them into the great Name of IHV, and with this He sealed the universe in the six directions.

Fifth He looked above and sealed the Height with IHV.

Sixth He looked below, and sealed the Depth with IVH.

Seventh He looked before Him and sealed the East with HIV.

Eighth He looked behind and sealed the West with HVI.

Ninth He looked to the right and sealed the South with VIH.

Tenth He looked to the left and sealed the North with VHI.

10. Behold, from the Ten Ineffable Sephiroth proceed the One Spirit of the Gods of living Air, Water, Fire, and Height, Depth, East, West, North, and South.
(assembled from various translations)

A BRIEF COMMENTARY ON THE VERSES:

1. The universal Being is defined, or we should say more accurately defines itself, by various names, which in themselves are states, stages, and divine entities; the titles are not mere praises or idle honorifics, but precise definitions and aspects of divinity. Perhaps the most obvious detail for the modern reader is that divinity is *plural*: from a single Being multiple divinities emanate.

Three modes of manifestation are technically defined in the ancient text: *Numbers, Letters, Sounds.* We find the use of number, letter (*shape with inherent power and meaning*) and sound in many variants of creation mythology. Obvious examples in our other chapters include Plato's *Myth of Er* (page 83) and the Pawnee creation myth (page 100).

The Sepher Yetzirah, however, is extremely precise in its application and combination of numbers, letters and sounds, for they are rooted in an ancient Kabbalistic tradition of instruction and enlightenment. The *Thirty-Two Paths* referred to are the ten stages (Spheres) and twenty-two links or combinations (Paths) of universal energy found upon the Tree of Life (see Figure 5). Thus we have originative divinity engraving its identity, Name, through three modes (numbers, letters, sounds) to define thirty-two Paths of Wisdom. The Paths represent the totality of the created and manifested universe, so the first verse takes us through the entire creation from Origination to Manifestation. The verses which follow elaborate upon each stage of the process.

2. The Ten Spheres of the Tree of Life, or *Sephiroth* , also translatable as *Ten Voices* or utterances from the void or chaos, are the major stages of universal manifestation, from the Void itself, through to the material substance. The Twenty Two Letters (of the Hebrew sacred alphabet) are allocated to the Paths or connections between each Sphere. If we use the analogy of utterance or voices for the Spheres, the Paths are the interactive resonance between them; once again this theory is defined by Plato, possibly drawing upon a Pythagorean creation myth. Although the system of the *Sepher Yetzirah* is more complex than that of Plato, they are clearly related to one another upon a fundamental level.

3. The number Ten is reaffirmed, and is shown to relate to the creation of the human body, which is a mirror or harmonic of the universal body.

4. The mystical power of the Ten Spheres or Utterances is affirmed as a route towards enlightenment and universal perfection.

5. The text now proceeds with the allocation of metaphysical Directions: a typical theme in creation mythology throughout the world. The Ten Voices or Utterances (Spheres shown on the Tree of Life) each have a vast region attuned or bonded to their resonance; these regions are defined or attuned but are without physical boundary. The map is that of Above/Below/East/West/South/North, giving the familiar Six Directions (see Figure 2).

Ten zones are defined in the verse as follows:

I Boundless Origin
II Endless (Time)
III Good (positive power potential)
IV Evil (negative power potential)
V Measureless Height
VI Measureless Depth
VII East

VIII West
IX North
X South

They are linked in pairs:

1. Boundless Origin/Endless (Time)
2. Good/Evil
3. Measureless Height/Depth
4. East/West
5. North/South

These pairs or polarities of Being may be further interpreted as:

1. (Pre-Time) Time
2. Energy (events)
3. Space
4 and 5 further 'engrave' or define interactions (events) within space and time.

We may now return to verse 6:

The Lightning Flash is the traditional shape or symbol of spiritual power taught in mystical instruction: it flashes 'down' the Tree of Life, in the order 1–2–3–4–5–6–7–8–9 –10. This primal Tree of Life pattern is found on the earliest illustrations, and the more complex Paths and Abyss pattern found in modern texts is generally a later development. Philosophically and mathematically, this tenfold utterance or energy pattern is related to that of the Pythagorean *Tetractys*, in which ten points of unfolding number or creation form a triangular pattern, (1 point at the crown, then 2 equidistant below it, then 3 below the 2, and 4 below 3, totalling 10). The Tetractys and the Tree of Life are variants of one another.

The Voices, however, emanate and return without end: the apparently linear sequence is a property of our limited field of awareness. The original Word, the first utterance of Being from Non-Being, is inherent within the Ten Voices. The imagery is that of a whirlwind or vortex of utterances or energies: in traditional terms they are also deities, the multiple forms and names of God.

7. This verse again affirms the ultimate Unity of Being. It also refers to certain mystical techniques of arousing energy within the human organism, which are said to be a reflection of the universal forces of creation.

8. The instructional and devotional tone of verse seven is given a definite form in verse eight: this refers to a specific meditational technique in which the human consciousness is brought into resonance with the primal Being or universal consciousness. Mythically, this is the re-creation of the Universe.

9. The text now proceeds to enumerate and define further stages of Creation, progressing to those of Number. The first Number, One, is that of the Living Spirit.

10. The second Number, Two, derives from One, and is the spiritual element of Air. Within this spiritual Air are shaped the twenty-two letters (Paths), which are allocated to those of the Hebrew alphabet. Thus language and writing are in themselves sacred and magical, for they constantly reiterate or re-create the universe.

Third, from Air, the Waters are shaped. (These are the stages of Creation referred to in the Book of Genesis in the Christian Old Testament, drawing upon ancient Hebrew sources.) Within this third phase, the material Foundation is shaped, which will become the manifested worlds of matter. This is the Ninth Sphere upon the Tree of Life.

Fourth, from Water, Fire is shaped. The Wheels, Flaming Serpents, and Holy Living Creatures are archangelic and angelic entities, referred to in the Vision of Ezekiel and other mystical texts. These entities of pure force define and delimit and enable all energies within the Universe, leading to the Foundation of form. This phase of creation, therefore, mirrors the polarised patterns, stated in the earlier verses, but always in increasingly specific forms.

The next stage of creation describes the allocation of rotations or cycles of the divine Name to the Four Directions. This *sealing* creates an abstract cube with six faces, within the universal unlimited sphere of Being.

The divine force, however, is not traditionally regarded as 'abstract' but as a living presence: in Kabbalistic mysticism each rotation of a divine name causes different combinations of energy to arise and resonate. It is upon this level of mystical perception that creation myth becomes aligned to practical magic, visualisation, and ritual pattern-making.

From the *Sepher Yetzirah* we now move to another famous cosmological text involving a sophisticated yet primal myth; this is found in the writings of Plato.

11. PLATO'S MYTH OF ER

The Myth of Er the Armenian, in Plato's *Republic*, has perplexed and delighted scholars for centuries, fusing as it does astronomy, musical symbolism, psycho-pompic tuition, and the ancient goddess orientated religion of the Mediterranean cultures. Whatever Plato's source, this complex vision, described as the near-death experience of Er, who seemed to die but returned to life again to recount his astonishing experience in great detail, includes a detailed cosmology. It is built upon a highly sophisticated creation myth, for it describes the structure, resonances, landscapes, and personae of the universe and how such resonances or archetypes reappear in the solar system. It then follows the universal series of reflections right through to human rebirth and transmigration of souls according to their inner or spiritual state of relative development, moral condition or, more rare, intentional choice guided by wisdom. The Myth of Er is, therefore, a very technical and complete vision, viewing the creation as an entity or system within which human spiritual development arises or degenerates.

In our present context we should concentrate primarily

on the cosmology and the mythic personae of the goddesses who hold the harmonies of the creation in resonant tension with one another. Joined to this traditional teaching, however, is a typical psycho-pompic or post-mortem vision, combined with precise instructions for the passage of the soul through the worlds after death, and so leading up to rebirth. The progressions described are detailed and specific, and clearly derive from a Mystery teaching, similar in purpose to a number of spiritual or initiatory 'guidebooks' such as Tibetan or Egyptian Books of the Dead, and other texts and traditions found worldwide. As the passage of the dead through the worlds, stellar, human, and underworld, is linked inseparably to the cosmology and powers of the universe, it forms a specific branch of creation mythology in its own right.

The translation which follows is based upon that of Thomas Taylor.

I will tell of a brave man, Er the son of Armenius, by descent a Pamphylian; who happened on a time to die in battle. When the dead were on the tenth day carried off, already corrupted, he was taken up and found still fresh; and being carried home, as he was about to be buried on the twelfth day, when laid upon the funeral pile he revived; and being revived he told what he saw in the other world. He said that after his soul left the body it went with many others, and that they came to a certain mysterious place where there were two chasms in the earth, near to each other, and two other openings in the heavens opposite to them. The judges (of the dead) sat between these openings.

And when they gave judgement they commanded the just to go to the right hand and upwards through the heavens, fixing before them symbols of the judgement pronounced; but the unjust they commanded to the left and downwards, and these, likewise, had behind them evidences of all that they had done. But on Er coming before the judges, they said it behoved him to be a messenger to mortal men concerning things in that place, and they commanded him to hear, and to contemplate everything in that place.

And he saw the souls departing through the two openings, some in one through the heavens, and some through one in the earth after they were judged. And through the other two openings he saw, rising through the one in the earth, souls full of squalidness and dust; and through the other he saw souls descending pure from the heavens, and always on their arrival they seemed as if they came from a long journey, and gladly went to rest themselves in the meadow, as if in a public assembly, and saluted one another, such as were acquainted. And those who rose up out of the earth asked the others concerning the things above, and those from the heavens asked them concerning the things below, and so they talked to one another. One type of soul wailing and weeping whilst they called to mind what and how many things they suffered and saw in their journey under earth, for it was a journey of a thousand years, and the others from the heavens explained their enjoyments and visions of immense beauty . . .

He also added, that every one, after they had been seven days in the meadow, arising thence, it was requisite for them to depart on the eighth day, and arrive at another place on the fourth day after, whence they perceived from above through the whole heaven and earth, a light extended as a pillar, mostly resembling the rainbow, but more splendid and pure; at which they arrived in one day's journey; and they perceived, being in the middle of the light from heaven, that its extremities were fastened to the sky. For this light was the belt of heaven, like the transverse beams of ships, and kept the whole circumference united. To the extremities the distaff of Necessity is fastened, by which all the revolutions of the world were made, and its spindle and point were both of adamant, but its whirl mixed of this and of other things; and that the nature of the whirl was of such kind, as to its figure, as is any one we see here. But you must conceive it, from what he said, to be of such a kind as this: as if in some great hollow whirl, carved throughout, there was such another, but lesser, within it, adapted to it, like casks fitted one within another; and in the same manner a third, and a fourth, and four others, for that the whirls were eight in all, as circles one within another, each having its rim appearing above the next; the whole forming round the spindle the united solidity of one whirl. The spindle was driven through the middle of the eight; and the first and outmost whirl had the widest circumference, the sixth had the next greatest width; the fourth the third width; then the eighth; the seventh; the fifth; and the second. Likewise the circle of the largest is variegated in colour; the seventh is the brightest, and that of the eighth hath its colour from the shining of the seventh; that of the second and fifth resemble each other, but are more yellow than the rest. But the third hath the whitest colour, the fourth is reddish; the second in whiteness surpasses the sixth. The distaff must turn round in a circle with the whole it carries; and whilst the whole is turning round, the seven inner circles are gently turned round in a contrary direction to the whole. Again, the eighth moves the swiftest; and next to it, and equal to one another, the seventh, the sixth, and the fifth; and the third went in a motion which as appeared to them completed its circle in the same way as the fourth, which in swiftness was the third, and the fifth was the second in speed. The distaff was turned round on the knees of Necessity. And on each of its circles there was seated a Siren on the upper side, carried round, and uttering one note in one tone. But that the whole of them, being eight, composed one harmony. There were other three sitting round at equal distances one from another, each on a throne, the daughters of Necessity, the Fates, in white vestments, and having crowns on their heads; Lachesis, and Clotho, and Atropos, singing to the harmony of the Sirens; Lachesis singing the past, Clotho the present, and Atropos the future. And Clotho, at certain intervals, with her right hand laid hold of the spindle, and along with her mother turned about the outer circle. And Atropos, in like manner, turned the inner ones with her left hand. And Lachesis touched both of these, severally, with either hand. Now after the souls arrive here, it is necessary for them to go directly to Lachesis, and then an herald first of all ranges them in order, and afterwards taking the lots, and the models of lives, from the knees of Lachesis, and ascending a lofty tribunal, he says: 'The speech of the virgin Lachesis, the daughter of Necessity. Souls of a day! This is the beginning of another period of men of mortal race. Your destiny shall not be given you by lot, but you should choose it yourselves. He who draws the first, let him first make choice of a life, to which he must of necessity adhere. Virtue is independent, which every one shall partake of, more or less, according as he honours or dishonours her. The cause is in him who makes the choice, and God is blameless!' When he had said these things, he threw on all of them the lots, and that each took up the one which fell beside him, but Er was allowed to take none. And that when each had taken it, he knew what number he had drawn.

After all the souls had chosen their lives according to the lots that they drew, they all went in order to Lachesis, and she gave to every one the fate that had been chosen by lot, and sent it along with them to be the guardian of their lives, and the accomplisher of what had been chosen. First of all he (the guardian) conducts the soul to Clotho, to ratify under her hand, and by the whirl of the vortex of her spindle, the destiny the soul had chosen by lot. And after being with her the guardian leads the soul back again to the spinning of Atropos, who makes the destinies irreversible. And from hence they proceed directly under the throne of Necessity; and after the others had passed by this throne, Er also passed, and they all of them marched into the plain of Lethe (Forgetfulness) amidst dreadful heat and scorching, for he said that it is void of trees and everything that the earth produces.

Then, when the night came on, they encamped beside the river Amelete (Indifference) whose water no vessel can contain. Of this water all of them must necessarily drink a certain measure, and such of them as are not preserved by prudence drink more than the measure, and he who drinks always forgets everything. But after they were laid down asleep, and it came to midnight, there was thunder, and an earthquake. They were thence of a sudden carried upwards, some one way, and some another, approaching to generation like stars. But Er himself was forbidden to drink of the water. Where, however, and in what manner, he came into his body, he was entirely ignorant; but suddenly waking up in the morning found himself already laid on the funeral pile.

And this fable has been preserved (by tradition) and is not lost, and so may it preserve us if we are persuaded by its wisdom; for thus may we pass over the river Lethe and our souls not be contaminated.

This remarkable myth, preserved by Plato at the closing of his *Republic* (written c.380 BC), could command an entire book of interpretation and comparison in its own right. The extracts given above contain the main themes and elements of the myth, and omit various details concerning rebirth, transmigration of souls, and moral lessons concerning evil, tyranny, and folly (supported by contemporary political and satirical allusions).

The perceptive reader will soon realise that the structure of Er's experience in the worlds beyond physical death is similar to the model of the Three Worlds: Heavens (stars), Earth (or middle world) and Underworld. The souls of living creatures rotate in an apparently endless cycle between the worlds, according to inevitable judgements passed upon them which lead to their own willing choice of lots for impending future lives.

A number of very detailed and informative esoteric teachings are included in the myth of Er, many of which are still found in the psychology of magical, meditative and spiritual disciplines to this day. But of direct interest is the description of the structures of the universe.

After a passage through an intermediate after-death state, leading to judgement and a vision of souls descending and ascending, Er travels to 'another place' in which a cosmic overview is gained. Firstly a rainbow (chromatic) pillar of light is seen, extended through heaven and earth. Upon reaching the middle of that light, they see that its extremities are 'fastened to the sky'. It is the belt of heaven which, like the transverse beam of a ship, keeps the whole circumference united. This pillar or belt of light is the universal beam or axis, often said to be represented by the Milky Way. The cosmology is that of a circle or sphere, with a unifying principle of light tying the universe together, held in balance just as an ancient Greek ship was held together (and pushed into shape) by its transverse beam.

To the extremities of this beam of light, Er saw fastened the distaff of Arete, Goddess of Necessity. Through this distaff the revolutions of the world (by which is meant both the universal and the planetary world) are generated. Necessity is the ancient Weaver Goddess, whose distaff blends forces into form, and from whose multi-coloured thread the Fates weave the tapestry of time, space and events. The distaff has points of adamant, we are told, but its *whirl* or *whorl* (the weighted end which gives weight to generate the spin that twines loose wool into thread) is of a mixture of materials, looking 'as to its figure' like a domestic distaff whorl 'as is any one we see here'. This intriguing vision is all the more significant when we remember that spiralling nebulae were not to be seen or represented for thousands of years by physical or materialist sciences.

Up to this stage we have a cosmic pattern: a universal sphere held in a balanced tension by a pillar or pivot of chromatic light; with an anthropomorphic vision of the creative and destructive forces, in the shape of a Weaver Goddess spinning thread out of the stuff of cosmic Being.

Next follows a description of the planetary motions and orbits, showing how the planets of our solar system travel within certain patterns relating to the orbits of one another. The image employed is of casks or spheres fitted proportionally within one another, and persisted as series of mathematical or geometrical figures in many variants as philosophers and scientists developed increasingly detailed models of the planetary orbits. (See the creative vision technique described by Plotinus on page 25 for a comparable parallel to this psycho-pompic cosmic vision, developed in visualising meditative techniques.)

Thus from the universal sphere, we have moved to the specific sphere of the planets in our solar system. The seven inner whirlings of spheres are the orbits of Saturn, Jupiter, Mars, Venus, Mercury, the Sun and the Moon. The outer varicoloured whirl or sphere is that of the starry universe. It is in this context that we have the famous musical model of the solar system, in which Sirens utter notes for each planetary orbit.

The three Fates, Lachesis, Clotho, and Atropos, the daughters of the Great Goddess, respectively sing (that is, 'utter or emit in resonance and harmony with one another') the past, present and future. The present, in the shape of Clotho, turns the universal sphere along with her mother using her right hand. This is the eternal present, Being, rotating into increasing manifestation. It shows that Being is ever present, timeless, and that our concept of the present is a transient reflection of an eternal or transcendent truth. The inner planetary spheres or orbits, however, are touched by the left hand of Atropos, singing the future. This counterbalances the universal energy, and generates a difference between present and future within the spheres of manifestation: time is a phenomenon of stellar and planetary forces in polarised patterns. Lachesis, singing the past, touches both outer and inner spheres with both hands, completing the generation or apparent pattern of time.

It is to the goddess of the past that the souls of the dead first come, for it is the energies of their past lives that will mould or impress patterns for their future rebirth. The rest of the myth deals with the soul's progress towards rebirth and the almost inevitable forgetting of the spiritual worlds.

Plato's writing spawned a vast horde of Neo-Platonic texts through the centuries, and now we may briefly examine Creation as described by Philo of Alexandria.

12. PHILO OF ALEXANDRIA

Philo of Alexandria (circa 20 BC to AD 50) made a remarkable fusion of Jewish and Hellenist philosophy and metaphysics in his copious writings. He was deeply influenced by the concepts of Plato and the subsequent developments of middle Platonist tradition, influenced by Stoicism and neo-Pythagorean thought. Yet he determined to merge this essentially Greek perennial wisdom, rooted in the primal myths described in our earlier chapters and in Plato's Myth of Er with the complex vast and profound mystical and religious traditions of his Jewish ancestors. So embedded in Jewish tradition that he wrote many of his Platonist treatises as exegeses upon the Pentateuch, Philo remains a subject of dissent and alternative theory among scholars to this day. In our present context a short extract will demonstrate the general ambience of his Jewish-Hellenistic texts dealing with the creation. As a fusion of Greek and Jewish traditions has contributed immensely to the development of Western culture, Philo's writings form an important set of threshold texts for further study.

(Her.134,140)

1. The Artificer took this substance and began to divide as follows: first he made two sections, the heavy and the light, separating the dense from the rare. He then divided again these two parts; the rare into air and fire, the dense into water and earth. These visible elements he laid down as an advance foundation of the visible world.

2. Thus did God sharpen his all-incisive Logos and divide the Universal Being which was without form and without quality, and the four elements of the world were separated off from it, and the animals and plants constituted from these.

We may now move to some examples of American Indian mythology to find that they are very similar indeed to the (supposedly) more civilised philosophy of Plato or the Neo-Platonists.

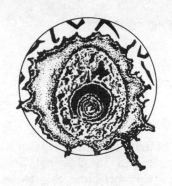

13.North American Indian Mythology

Until quite recently, it was commonly assumed that the religion and mythology of the various races of North American Indians was primitive totemism, and that the people themselves were little more than savages. Today this untruth has been shattered, and despite the virtual destruction of the original Indian races by the white, much of Indian religion, myth, and magic still remains. Some of the current interest in native American lore is, unfortunately, ephemeral and fashionable, but it is clear that the deeper traditions may still be worked as powerful magical or imaginative systems in their own right. As in all the summaries of mythology offered in this book, the following is only a general listing of concepts to show the basic relationship between North American Indian mythology and that of other races or lands. The examples chosen are merely a tiny portion out of the vast storehouse of native American myth and legend.

FOREST INDIAN MYTHOLOGY

The cosmology of the forest Indians is similar in a number of ways to that found in classical Greek, Roman, or Celtic myth. We may presume this to be a property of consciousness, and must certainly not fall into the trap of suggesting that there is any 'original' mythic sequence carried from place to place.

Having said as much, there may be a connection between native American culture and that of Europe and the Mediterranean to the east across the Atlantic Ocean: Professor Barry Fell and others have repeatedly proposed and offered evidence that, contrary to popular assumption, people did cross the ocean in ancient times. Evidence deriving from stone structures and debatably ancient inscriptions in America suggests that there were Celtic settlements upon the Eastern seaboard up to the first century BC or even later, and that Libyan, Egyptian, and Carthaginian contacts were also maintained. It is not the place or aim of this book to argue such matters, merely to state their existence. (See Barry Fell, *America BC*, and other books, published by Pocket Books, USA.)

Whatever the connections, the North American Indians preserved a traditional cosmology which is basically shared, with variations, worldwide. This includes concepts of space, time, creative and destructive forces and entities, which are far indeed from primitive superstition. Upon analysis they are found to be more aligned conceptually to the perennial philosophy or metaphysics represented by Plato or Pythagoras than to any outmoded concept of hard-primitivism such as was once applied to the native peoples of America by ignorant European scholars and religious propagandists.

The basic cosmology of tribes such as the Algonquins, for example, employs the model of the Four Directions and Four Elements. There are four upper worlds or dimensions, mirrored by four lower. This is, in essence, the spherical metaphysics of creation mythology in general . . . a property of human consciousness seeking intuitive approaches to Being. Four spiritual entities inhabit the Four Directions: North is the abode of a Winter spirit, connected to hunting and animals, while South is that of a Summer spirit, connected to crops and fruitfulness. West is the realm of water and rainfall, while East brings sunlight and brightness. These are, in essence, familiar concepts of the Four Elements of Air and Spring (East), Fire and Summer (South), Water and Autumn (West), and Earth and Winter (North), they are shown in Figure 3.

Weather is under the control of the Thunder Bird, who is attended by lesser spirits in the form of raptors. This mythic bird, whose wing-beats are the thunder claps and whose eyes radiate lightning, is found throughout most Indian legends.

The clouds above (using the ubiquitous model of the Six Directions as in our Figure 2) are the realm of beings of wind and thunder, while higher still are the Sun and Moon, often represented as brother and sister. Above the Sun and Moon again are the living stars. The planet Earth, or the Land below, is represented by a Mother goddess, whom the Algonquin Indians call *Nokomis*, Grandmother.

As in all primal mythologies, the zones and entities of creation are linked by specific animals, who act as intermediaries between human beings upon the Earth, and other dimensions and beings. Birds traditionally act as links to the airy worlds, while reptiles or serpents and fish link to the underworld. We find this simple (but by no means childish) model underpinning most mythologies. Totem beasts are so important that they even persist into orthodox religions of the world (including Christianity), in which major deities, saints and holy men and women are accompanied or represented by specific creatures.

All created entities are endowed with a primal power, called *Manitou* by the Algonquins or *Orenda* by the Iroquois. Lesser entities or Manitous may come under the control of humanity, while the great Manitous are potent self-motivated spiritual entities. The Great Spirit, or *Kitcki Manitou* of the Algonquins is a transcendent uncreated spiritual Being. Its totem creature is a great white bird, sent as messenger to humanity.

The Great Spirit is the breather forth of life, present in all things through the pervasive movement of the four winds; it is made manifest in the light of the sun, the physical sun being both a deity and a representative form of a spiritual transcendent principle of Light. We have used the term 'it' for the Great Spirit, in the sense of transcending sexuality or polarity, but it is often identified in myth and legend as male.

The Arapahoe Indians describe Kitcki Manitou as the ancestor of the sacred pipe; before the world was created he wandered over a vast watery waste, crying and fasting, seeking the place where the earth would rise into being. He called upon the creatures which already existed, water birds and reptiles, to help him in his quest. The turtle was able to locate the earth below the cosmic waters, and the water birds brought its clay back in their beaks. Kitcki Manitou dried this clay upon his pipe, and so made the manifest world. Thus the familiar Indian ceremony of communal pipe smoking is a ritual re-creating the world, a mythic drama or ceremony of regeneration and unity.

The Algonquin Indians also have legends of an ancestral spirit, the Great Hare, *Michabo*, who created the earth, water and many animals. This spirit inhabits the region of the dawn, and the souls of humans are under its special protection.

THE IROQUOIS AND HURON INDIANS

Iroquois mythology defines a titanic race of beings, very similar in function to those of the Ancient Greeks, and of the type found in most primal or early levels of creation myth . . . a pre-human race with awesome powers. As is often the case, these titanic beings are merged in the collective tradition with ancestral beliefs. We find similar themes from mythologies as distant as that of the Jews, now incorporated into the Old Testament, but there is no implication in this similarity (as some eccentric writers have suggested) that the native American Indians are, in fact, the lost tribes of Israel, any more than the Titans and Giants in Greek or Celtic mythology imply a similar connection.

The giants are in control of elemental forces, Wind, Thunder, and Echo. Wind is ruled by *Ga-oh*, while thunder is ruled by *Hino*, the sky-guardian. As with all titanic forces and entities in mythology, these early created beings may be malefic if offended or improperly invoked, or beneficial if understood and related to in a balanced manner. The Thunder spirit, armed with bow and fiery arrows, is essentially a purifier or destroyer of negative harmful forces and forms.

Such spirits are important in the transformative magical arts, by which the magician may be either broken and destroyed or purified and transformed into a new form or level of awareness. Much of Indian mythology has this heroic undertone. The Thunder spirit is partnered by a female spirit of the Rainbow, and assisted by a mortal child transformed into immortality, *Gunnodoyak*. This human-divine child fought the great devouring serpent or Water Snake, but despite being defeated was resurrected and carried to the heavens when Hino and his spirit warriors themselves finally destroyed the Serpent. In this legend we may find many parallels to those of other societies or races.

The Western quarter of the sky is the realm of *Oshadagea*, the Great Eagle of Dew. This bird, associated with the Thunder spirit Hino, brings beneficial moisture to the earth by spreading rain or dew from his beating wings to disperse drought. Upon his back is a lake of dew.

The Iroquois preserve a tradition similar to that of ancient Greece, in which a maiden of fruitfulness is carried off to the Underworld. The Earth Mother, *Eithinoha* had a daughter, *Onatha*. Onatha, Spirit of Grain, travelled forth to find Dew, but was captured by a dark spirit who trapped her under the earth. Eventually she was liberated by the return of the sun. While this type of story is often regarded as a 'vegetation myth' based upon seasonal observation of the cycles of sun and harvest, winter and spring, it has an important role in the preservation of creation myth also. The locations employed are the basic three: natural world, heavenly world, and underworld. The vegetation or fertility myth defines these locations very clearly.

THE SELISH MYTHOLOGY

One of the oldest Indian nations is that of the Selish: their creation mythology, like a number of others, defines three worlds: the heavens, the earth (or land), and the underworld. Through the centre of the worlds or planes is a vast pole or world tree. Certain Indian myths involve the toppling of this pole or pillar-tree, and as a cosmological or astrological/astronomical feature, this theme is found in many variants worldwide. It has been suggested, both by modern writers and in esoteric tuition circulated within limited groups or societies since ancient times, that toppling and replacement of the world-tree is from a tradition connected to stellar phenomena observed over immense periods of time. In a metaphysical sense it represents the unfastening or unhinging of one cycle of creation and the establishment of a new order. In a physical stellar sense it refers to alterations in the planetary orbit which cause changes in the patterns of stars observed in the sky. Such alteration may be slow and established, such as the precession of the Equinoxes, or may be of a sudden catastrophic nature, as in the traditions of vanishing continents, great deluges, and other powerful changes wrought by planetary collision with comets, and so forth.

The ultimate deity of the Selish is *Amotken*, wise and benevolent, creator of all things. Typically, his messenger is Coyote, a mercurial figure who features strongly in Indian legend, sometimes as a malevolent trickster travelling between the worlds, at other times as a bringer of knowledge and illumination. Amotken made five female beings from the hair of his head, and asked them what they willed. One became mother of goodness, and another mother of evil. The third became the mother of earth, while the fourth became the mother of fire. The fifth became the mother of water. The concept of Three Mothers, relating to three primal elements, permeates creation mythology, and is found in many ancient traditions. Thus we have an increasingly polarised or manifesting pattern of energies: positive and negative (good and evil) and the pattern of the elements, leading to the appearance of individual creatures which move and respond to the primal forces or goddesses.

THE ZUNI CREATION MYTH

Far to the south, we find that the Pueblo Zuni Indians preserve a complex cosmic myth of the creation, which may be summarised thus:

The original creator was a bisexual or transcendent deity, *Awonawilona*. By will this primal undifferentiated being emitted mists and streams of growth and moisture. This primal sea developed green scum, enlivened by the light of the sun also emitted by the primal Being. Eventually the earth mother, *Awitilin Tsta* and the sky father *Apoyan Tachi* separated out of the primal sea and slime, making the created world.

The Earth Mother had a quadruple womb, in which proto-beings were formed: out of one of these wombs came the first human or original ancestor, *Poshaiyangkyo*. He prayed to Awonawilona to liberate the unformed creatures in the earth mother's quadruple womb; in response she created a pair of immortal twins who divided the substance of the earth with thunderbolts and by descending upon spiderwebs entered into the primal fourfold womb. The beings that they led out into the light populated the land, but those that fell behind became monsters.

This very complete myth, of which the foregoing is only a brief summary, leads us progressively from a pre-planetary condition, to the material creation, and then gives a clear picture of what a modern scientist might call 'evolution', though in keeping with all ancient traditions the concept is directly dependent upon divine creation rather than blind trial and error. The image of the four wombs or primal elements appears once again, and the completion of beings out of the wombs is dependent upon a further development or manifestation of the divine Being, this time as heavenly or energising twins. This theme, of a sacred child or children of light sent by the creator to advance, complete or redeem an earlier phase of creation, is widely found in mythology and religion throughout human culture and history.

MYTHOLOGY OF THE PLAINS INDIANS

The Indians of the great plains also held the tradition of the Great Spirit, a supreme being and creator, often called the Great Mystery. The Pawnees called this being *Tirawa*, the Arch of Heaven, a term also employed in Celtic tradition. Images for the creator were in terms of light, height, life, energy. The Sioux called the Great Spirit *Wakonda*, and from Wakonda emanated lesser gods and goddesses such as the Sun, the Moon, the Morning Star, the Elements, and of course Thunder.

A PAWNEE CREATION MYTH

This summary of a Pawnee creation myth follows the typical patterns of the Four Directions, the Stellar and planetary powers, and the manifesting world: The Great Spirit Tirawa and his consort Atira were in the starry sky. The lesser powers sat around them in a circle, and Tirawa said, 'I shall endow each of you with a share of my power and a function in the heavens, and I shall create humankind who shall be under your protection.' In the East the Great Spirit located *Shakuru*, the Sun, for light and heat by day, and in the West he located *Pah*, the Moon, to illuminate the darkness of night. The Evening Star he also set in the West, to be the mother of all created things, for she created all living beings. The warrior Morning Star he placed in the East, to ensure that none remained behind when they were sent to the West.

In the North Tirawa set the Pole Star, as the primary star of the heavens, and in the South he set the Death Star, the light of the ancestral spirits. Four other stars he placed in the positions of North East, North West, South East, and South West: these were the supporters of the sky. Then the Great Spirit sent clouds, winds, thunder and lightning towards the Evening Star, to begin the process of creation.

When the sky was dark with thunder, filled with rain and wind and lightning, Tirawa let a stone fall upon the cloud mantle, which parted asunder and revealed a vast stretch of water. The four powers of the Quarters struck the water with their staves or maces and separated the waters from the earth. Then Tirawa ordered the gods to begin singing in praise of his creation, and the sound of their voices brought the elements, the clouds, thunder, lightning and wind all together, generating a storm of the utmost terrible power. This great storm, drawn together by the song of the powers of the Quarters, caused the earth to split into high mountains and deep valleys.

Next the four powers sang in praise of trees and grassy plains, and a second great storm was generated, which made the earth green and covered with growing trees and plants. A third time they sang, and the flood of water from the storm filled the rivers and streams and caused them to flow. With their fourth chant, seeds sprang forth and germinated.

Then Tirawa commanded the Sun and Moon to mate, and they bore a son, and he commanded the Morning and Evening Stars to mate, and they bore a daughter. These divine children were placed upon the Earth, and the powers and gods taught them the secrets of nature. The woman learned the arts of fire, of speech, of hearth, planting, and home. The man received the weapons of a warrior, the names of all animals, and the skills of hunting. Bright Star taught the man the ritual of sacrifice, and he became first chief over all other men and women that were created, and taught them all his art and knowledge. They built a great circular camp, patterned after the order of the heavens, as a reflection and memorial of the creation of the world.

The Pawnee creation myth, briefly summarised above, has a number of intriguing motifs which are found in primal mythology elsewhere. The metaphysical concept of sound, and specifically chanting or musical intonation as a creative force, is preserved in many esoteric traditions from the ancient world. Of particular note also is the tradition that the first race of humans built their camp in a circle, modelled upon the map of the heavens. This modelling of the land and human society upon mythic and stellar archetypes and patterns is a persistent theme in early societies, ranging from the vast structures of the Babylonian or Egyptian civilisations, to the traditional divisions of land and castes such as we find in India, and again in the heroic poetry and legends of ancient Ireland.

The Pawnee circular camp, with its ancestral chieftain teaching skills, initiated by the gods into the ritual of sacrifice, is echoed exactly in the concept of sacred kingship which underpinned religion in ancient Europe and Asia. Sacred kingship and an archetypical pattern on earth that reflects the creative perfection of heaven is, of course, closely related to the foundations of Arthurian legend and the origins of the Round Table.

This transatlantic harmony with Arthurian tradition leads us to Celtic creation mythology. We may now turn to the Merlin legends, which hold a comprehensive myth of creation.

14. THE VISION OF
MERLIN AND TALIESIN
FROM THE 12TH CENTURY
VITA MERLINI

Although the *Vita Merlini* is the biography of Merlin, it is assembled from a loose collection of separate poems, tales, motifs, all woven around Merlin as the central character. It has a large detailed section on creation and cosmology, ranging from the origin of the universe, to the appearance of the planet Earth. The text then meanders through the created orders of beings, and becomes a natural history text. But it does not become a mere catalogue of beasts, birds and fishes, we always realise that these lists are attuned to the original pattern of the Four Powers or Elements (see Figure 3). The creation episode of the text then transports the reader to the Otherworld Islands, the mysterious spiritual realms or innerworld of the Celts.

The basic pattern is shown in Figure 7, and consists of five interlinked spheres or rings. This cosmic pattern has its mirror in the planet Earth, with its five zones, four winds, great rivers, and circulatory system of weather.

Figure 7 The Creation Vision

The Creation Vision of the 12th century *Vita Merlini* is a fusion of bardic Celtic (Welsh or Breton) tradition, with Greek and orthodox religious elements. It is not, significantly, a typically orthodox creation myth or cosmogony, and its curious features are likely to be due to its derivation from creation poems in bardic tradition. It represents a classic model of Creation as it was understood in the ancient world, but refined and preserved through the literary work of Geoffrey of Monmouth, who wrote the *Vita Merlini* in approximately 1150.

It shows a creation pattern as follows:

1. Four Elements or Powers are uttered by Divinity.
2. These are reiterated through the realms of the stars and planets.
3. They then form the Four Elements, Four Winds, and Four Zones of the planet Earth.

Every Fourfold cycle is within or connected by a Fifth or spiritual element, giving an overall image of five circles interlinked. This fivefold pattern devolves or manifests through each of the Three Worlds, acting as an archetypical pattern or mould for the creation of entities and life forms in each World: Stellar, Solar, and Lunar. The Lunar World includes the planet Earth.

The orders of beings, angels, spirits, daemones, humanity, are further complemented by birds, fishes, beasts, and serpents, and the qualities of the various planetary zones are described in detail in the original text.

The *Creation Vision* also describes how the cycles of weather, such as wind and rain, are an inherent property of the Fourfold Pattern of the universe, for all events are due to rotations and combinations of pattern deriving from the Four Elements. The overall effect is that of vast organic interconnected Creation, with rhythms and movement to and fro between the worlds, and all created zones and beings harmonically related to one another. It was this type of holistic image that was to become subtly altered into the concept of the universe as a 'great machine' which appeared in the eighteenth century, and persists in an attenuated form even today. Modern physics, however, is far closer to the cosmic vision of the *Vita Merlini* than science has ever been since the eighteenth century, so the pattern, as indicated by the Creation Vision itself, has turned a full cycle.

The entire creation text, as recited to Merlin by the bard Taliesin as a rather remarkable response to the question 'Why do we have such bad weather?' is carefully structured and well defined; it may be one of the few remaining sources for druidic cosmology as it is very likely that Geoffrey of Monmouth developed his material from verses recited by the bards and story-tellers of Brittany or Wales. Such travelling poets preserved the remnants of the old druidic system which had long been officially banned (since the days of the Roman presence in Britain and Gaul) but had remained as a poetic tradition for over a thousand years. In Ireland, of course, the druidic religion persisted well into the Christian period, as the Romans did not conquer Ireland, and it remained to the Church to remove the religious elements of druidism while retaining the poetic and hierarchical traditions upon which the Celtic culture was founded. When we consider the patterns defined by the *Vita Merlini* we find them to be typical creation patterns that appear in so many myths worldwide, regardless of historical time or place.

Before quoting directly from a translation of the text, the following summary will be helpful. The Creation Vision progress is as follows:

ELEMENTS AND CIRCLES

1. The four elements are produced from nothing.

2. They are joined in harmony by the creator.

3. Heaven is adorned with stars and surrounds the creation.

4. Air is created below the stars, as a medium for day and night.

5. The sea girds the land in four circles, and with its turning of tides (mighty refluence) generates:

6. The four winds.

7. The earth is made as a foundation (for the *Axis Mundi* or Pivot of the Worlds), and is divided into five zones.

The middle of the earth is too hot for life, the furthest north and south are too cold (the Arctic and Antarctic) but two moderate zones are suitable for life, and are inhabited by humanity, birds, and wild beasts.

CLOUDS, RAINS, AND WINDS

The operation of the weather is defined, with the action of the sun creating the circulation of water through evaporation and rain, while the winds partake of the nature of the zones in which they are born.

ORDERS OF SPIRITS

The entire creation is then recapitulated, and having established its pattern of zones through to the inhabitation of the planet, the spiritual entities that occupy the dimensions between the creator and the Earth are described.

1. The ethereal Heaven beyond the stars is occupied by angels who are refreshed through contemplating divinity.

2. The stars and the sun are given fixed paths.

3. The airy heavens are created beneath the stars and Sun, and occupied by the Moon, and troops of spirits who sympathise and rejoice along with humankind. These entities carry prayers and dreams to and fro between the spiritual dimensions.

4. The sublunary world, between the airy heavens of the Moon and the planet Earth, are occupied by demons or *daemones*, which approach the physical manifestation, and even reach into sexuality.

The heavens therefore have three orders of spirits to perpetually renew the cyclical energies of the fivefold pattern.

From this detailed cosmology and spiritual geography, the text later goes on to describe the orders of animals, birds, and fishes, the divisions of the seas, and the magical islands, of which Britain is said to be the best. Finally, the tale leads to a mysterious otherworld, called the Fortunate Isle, ruled by a goddess or priestess, Morgen, who has powers of therapy and flight, supported by a mysterious group of seven sisters. She, we are informed, has the task of curing the mortally wounded King Arthur, whom – Merlin and Taliesin ferried to her domain after the terrible battle of Camlann.

ELEMENTS AND CIRCLES

Meanwhile Taliesin had come to see Merlin the prophet who had sent for him to find out what caused wind or rainstorms, for both together were drawing near and the clouds were thickening. He drew the following illustrations under the guidance of Minerva his associate.

'Out of nothing the Creator of the world produced *four elements* that they might be the prior cause as well as the material for creating all things when they were joined together in harmony: the *heaven* which He adorned with *stars* and which stands on high and embraces everything like the shells surrounding a nut; then He made the *air*, fit for forming sounds, through the medium of which day and night present the stars; the *sea* which girds the land in four circles, and with its mighty refluence so strikes the air as to generate the *winds* which are said to be four in number; as a foundation He placed the earth, standing by its own strength and not lightly moved, which is divided into five parts, whereof the middle one is not habitable because of the heat and the two furthest are shunned because of their cold. To the last two He gave a moderate temperature and these are inhabited by *men* and *birds* and herds of *wild beasts*.

CLOUDS, RAIN, WINDS

He added clouds to the sky so that they might furnish
sudden showers to make the fruits of the trees and of
the ground grow with their gentle sprinkling. With
the help of the sun these are filled like water skins
from the rivers by a hidden law, and then, rising
through the upper air, they pour out the water they
have taken up, driven by the force of the winds. From
them come rainstorms, snow, and round hail when
the cold damp wind breathes out its blasts which,
penetrating the clouds, drive out the streams just as
they make them. Each of the winds takes to itself a
nature of its own from its proximity to the zone where
it is born.

ORDERS OF SPIRITS

Beyond the firmament in which He fixed the shining
stars He placed the *ethereal heaven* and gave it as
a habitation to troops of *angels* whom the worthy
contemplation and marvellous sweetness of God re-
fresh throughout the ages. This also He adorned with
stars and the *shining sun*, laying down the law, by
which a star should run within fixed limits through
the part of heaven entrusted to it.

He afterwards placed beneath this the *airy heavens*,
shining with the lunary body, which throughout
their high places abound in troops of *spirits* who
sympathize or rejoice with us as things go well or
ill. They are accustomed to carry the prayers of men
through the air and to beseech God to have mercy on
them, and to bring back intimations of God's will,
either in dreams or by voice or by other signs, through
doing which they become wise.

The space below the moon abounds in evil
daemons,
who are skilled to cheat and deceive and tempt us;
often they assume a body made of air and appear to
us and many things often follow. They even hold

intercourse with women and make them pregnant, generating in an unholy manner. So therefore He made the heavens to be inhabited by *three orders of spirits* that each one might look out for something and renew the world from the renewed seed of things.

THE SEA

The sea too He distinguished by various forms that from itself it might produce the forms of things, generating throughout the ages. Indeed, part of it burns and part freezes and the third part, getting a moderate temperature from the other two, ministers to our needs.

That part which burns surrounds a gulf and fierce people, and its divers streams, flowing back, separate this from the orb of earth, increasing fire from fire. Thither descend those who transgress the laws and reject God; whither their perverse will leads them they go, eager to destroy what is forbidden to them. There stands the stern-eyed judge holding his equal balance and giving to each one his merits and his deserts.

The second part, which freezes, rolls about the foreshorn sands which it is the first to generate from the near-by vapour when it is mingled with the rays of Venus's star. This star, the Arabs say, makes shining gems when it passes through the Fishes while its waters look back at the flames. These gems by their virtues benefit the people who wear them, and make many well and keep them so. These too the Maker distinguished by their kinds as He did all things, that we might discern from their forms and from their colours of what kinds they are and of what manifest virtues.

The third form of the sea which circles our orb furnishes us many good things owing to its proximity. For it nourishes fishes and produces salt in abundance, and bears back and forth ships carrying our commerce, by the profits of which the poor man becomes suddenly rich. It makes fertile the neighbouring soil and feeds the birds who, they say, are generated from it along with the fishes and, although unlike, are moved by the laws of nature. The sea is dominated by them more than by the fishes, and they fly lightly up from it through space and seek the lofty regions. But its moisture drives the fishes beneath the waves and keeps them there, and does not permit them to live when they get out into the dry light. These too the Maker distinguished according to their species and to the different ones gave each his nature, whence through the ages they were to become admirable and healthful to the sick.

Having moved from the creation myths of early cultures and primal peoples into the remnants of Celtic cosmology in the Middle Ages, we may now make the last transition and consider how Creation Myth might be used today.

15.

CONTEMPORARY
VISUALISATION

The various examples from tradition described or quoted
in the preceding chapters should provide ample material
for those with some experience in meditation or visualisation, but as the range of techniques used today is so
wide, it is well worth restating some of the basic principles
which are inherent within creation mythology itself, and
their application to individual or group meditation and
visualisation. Before entering into examples, there are a
small number of important guiding comments, taking the
form of negatives.

NEGATIVES

Work with creation mythology and the imagination should
not be undertaken solely as a therapeutic exercise. If
therapy is considered as an end in itself, the true nature
of creation myth is misunderstood or even abused. There
are indeed many balancing or therapeutic effects from

visualising or meditating upon traditional creation patterns, but the end is the creation itself, not any individual (that is, separated) benefit that might occur through such work.

The same rule applies, perhaps more obviously, to attempts at false self-inflation. If we attempt to use creation imagery to make a false self-esteemed or self-orientated pseudo-world, then the results may be at best ineffectual, or at worst dangerous and unbalancing. There is a common fallacy, based on commercialised principles deriving from materialist psychology, that visualisation and the will may be applied 'to get what you want'. There is some truth in this rather superficial theory, but the correct approach was epitomised by the late Dion Fortune, one of the pioneers in restatement of esoteric psychology and magical arts for the twentieth century, who once said something similar to: 'Be careful in whatever you ask for, as you might receive it'.

Creation visualisation should not be imposed upon third parties, either willingly or unwillingly. In other words it is not advisable or ethical to use techniques which purport to send the images or energies over a distance, such as in absent healing, or to introduce individuals into groups conducting visualisations without their full understanding and participation.

The creation myths resonate to our deepest perceptions of reality, and therefore work upon levels of consciousness that may be shared, but not wilfully transferred. Perhaps contemplation would be a better term than meditation, as the individual passes through the visions built within the imagination (as in our classic example quoted from Plotinus on page 25), into a further formless state of awareness, through the use of creation patterns or myths.

POSITIVES

Visualisation and contemplation using creation imagery or patterns should always be accompanied by regular rhythmic breathing. In many traditions, the breath is said to be the physical expression of the life force, and a resonance of the universal breath that was first uttered forth from the void. The steady rhythm of breathing in and out forms an essential part of meditation, and acts as a grounding or steadying influence upon the organism. In later stages, the breath becomes a vehicle for higher forces, but this development belongs to more detailed esoteric training, and is not considered any further in our present context.

Dedication of space is very helpful to work with creation imagery. The unavoidable dedicated space is, of course, that occupied by our physical body. If possible we may also utilise a physical space such as a room, or even a small area surrounding the chair in which we sit. In advanced meditational or magical arts, the dedication and energising of a space becomes a major consideration, but for the present it should be that self-defined space which begins in the imagination, and extends to a field or sphere of awareness around us.

The philosophical basis for this is the realisation that the shape which encompasses all dimensions is that of an unlimited or expanding sphere. This is the type of concept central to ancient metaphysical texts on creation such as the *Sepher Yetzirah* (page 75), and which reappears in modern cosmology and physics. The dedication or re-attuning of space is based upon the directional model, in which the image of a standing human, upon the plane of the land or on the horizon, initially defines Above, Below, Before/East, Right/South, Behind/West, Left/North. In later stages any direction may be faced (Before), thus establishing a new relative orientation.

Work with creation imagery always begins from still-ness, silence, or peace. This is most vital reiteration of the cosmic process described in the myths themselves, for creation was uttered or manifested out of nothing, the void, silence, stillness. Thus there is a paradoxical but essential technique to master before any new creation may be truly effective: the consciousness must be stilled, the personal (relatively habitual) world must be dissolved, even if only temporarily. The approach to silence takes much

114

practice and discipline, but may be generally made by sitting quietly, breathing regularly, and gradually calming all random thought or emotion.

Thus the first part of any creation visualisation is to reach within oneself and be still, echoing that primal stillness and emptiness which creation myths state as the source of all subsequent Being.

Having briefly touched upon these negative and positive guidelines, the most important of which is that of approaching silence, let us proceed to some of the traditional methods themselves.

IMAGES

The time-hallowed method, and still the most powerful, is to work with picture images. These are usually taken from a creation narrative, and originally would have been known through verses, music, and dance, as part of a traditional body of knowledge. Sacred texts and verses were said to have great power and merit in themselves, and such texts often hold sequences of potent imagery which would have been part of meditation, prayer, or visualisation. But we must also remember that the ordinary tales and legends, part of communal tradition, were often keys into the primal realms of creation mythology.

It would still be highly effective for the student to learn (even in translation) a creation myth by heart before beginning any visualisation, but for basic work a summary may be made in writing. This summary should be taken from a good translation of a myth, or, less effectively, from a general description such as those given in our earlier chapters. It should always be based upon the images of major characters, and the progression of their interaction or story.

The summary of the mythic narrative is then further refined into essential sets of images, and these are visualised after the individual or group has spent some preliminary time in stillness and silence. The advantage of learning a tale or sequence by heart is that it unfolds very naturally within the imagination; another method would be to work with one person reading or reciting, or from a pre-recorded tape, perhaps with suitable music, to help attune the imagination to the subject.

The images are naturalistic: they involve beings, creatures, starscapes or landscapes, in an ordered progression according to the myth being entered. Turn, for example, to pages 49–50 on Greek mythology, for a simple summary of the creation of a primal god and goddess from the gaping emptiness of chaos. This could easily develop into a simple sequence for visualisation emerging from primal silence and stillness.

PURE FORMS

The 'Pure Forms' method, once widely used in mystical and metaphysical disciplines, but far harder to work with than that described above, employs geometric or mathematical forms. These so-called 'pure' forms are found in the Platonic solids, sets of shapes conceived as three-dimensional (or in even higher orders of dimension) within the imagination. Thus the meditator might pass from contemplating the void, to the appearance of a single point of light within that void. The light becomes a moving line which rotates and describes a circle: the circle is then realised as a sphere, and within it a cube is formed generating the relative directions. Further more complex solids are then imagined.

It is significant that many refined mystical creation patterns combine images and forms, for the naturalistic or anthropomorphic entities are part of, or an alternative expression of, the mathematical or geometric universal forms.

MIRRORING WITHIN THE IMAGINATION

There is common assumption that creation mythology or metaphysical techniques in general must be nebulous, vague, ethereal or extremely tenuous. This is far from the case, and as can be seen from the examples given in our earlier chapters, creation myths are strong, vibrant, and often sensuous or blatantly sexual. This does not simply imply that our ancestors laid all creation to the function of copulation, but that the universal creation was mirrored or harmonised by physical, sexual or generative forces, forms and patterns in nature.

It is possible to attune to the deepest forces of creation, according to poetic and mythic tradition, through the use of naturalistic imagery which mirrors those cosmic processes. It must be stressed that this is not identical to the use of allegory, in which sets of actions represent other actions by one remove or through similarities encoded in a formal convention. While allegory seems to play an important part in myth, this is really an impression generated by hindsight on our part. It would be correct to use the term 'resonance' rather than allegory: the sensuous myths resonate in harmony with transcendent patterns of universal creation.

Poets, of course, have known of this technique for millennia. Let us take an example from a relatively modern poet, William Sharp, who wrote under the name of Fiona Macleod, working within a Celtic tradition, and using sensuous imagery of a god and goddess in nature to create a mythic creation pattern. Imaginative work with this sequence resonates not only to the natural world, but the higher worlds or universe.

Midir In the days of the Great Fires when the hills were aflame,
Aed the Shining God lay by a foam-white mountain,
The White thigh of moon-crowned Dana, Beautiful Mother.
And the wind fretted the blue with the tossed, curling clouds
Of her tangled hair, and like two flaming stars were her eyes.

Torches of sunfire and moonfire: and her vast
  breasts
Heaved as the sea heaves in the great calms, and
  the wind of her sighs
Were as the winds of sunrise soaring the peaks of
  the eagles . . . .
Dana, Mother of Gods, moon-crowned, sea-shod,
  wonderful!
'Fire of my love,' she cried. Aed of the Sunlight
  and Shadow
Laughed: and he rose till he grew more vast than
  Dana:
The sun was his trampling foot, and he wore the
  white moon as a feather:
And he lay by Dana: and the world swayed, and
  the stars swung.
Thus was OEngus born, Lord of Love, Son of
  Wisdom and Death.

Eochaidh Hear us, OEngus, beautiful, terrible, Sun-Lord
  and Death-Lord!
Give us the white flame of love born of Aed and of
  Dana . . . .
Hearken, thou Pulse of hearts, and let the white
  doves from thy lips
Cover with passionate wings the silence between
  us,
Where a white fawn leaps and only Etain and I
  behold it.

From *The Immortal Hour*, Fiona Macleod

The poem quoted above was used by composer Rutland
Boughton in his setting of William Sharp's *Immortal Hour*,
which became one of the longest running operas of all
time. Creation myth may work through many levels, all
resonating to its most primal timeless source within a
tradition.

APPENDIX 1:

THE SEVEN APHORISMS

OF CREATION

The verses which follow were used for esoteric instruction by T.W. Moriarty, who was the original teacher of the well known twentieth-century writer on psychology and practical magic, Dion Fortune. We may consider them in two ways: firstly they could merely be poetic vehicles for cosmology and mysticism, assembled by the author during the early years of the twentieth century. As such they are firmly founded within the traditions of creation mythology, though bearing the mark of an individual within a modern culture. The second approach to these verses, which is certainly that taken by Moriarty and his pupils, is that they are a received or regenerated creation myth, a mystical text with its origins deep in the roots of consciousness, communicated to the human world from the mythic and potent otherworld. The final judgement may be left to individual intuition.

THE APHORISMS

1. The Eternal Parent was wrapped in the sleep of
    cosmic night,
    And nothing existed in manifestation, either real or
    apparent.
    Light there was not; for the flame of spirit had not
    been rekindled.
    Time there was not; for change had not yet re-begun.
    Things there were not; for Form had not yet re-
    presented itself.
    Action there was not; for there were no things to act.
    Polarity there was not; for there were no things to
    manifest opposites.
    The Eternal Parent, causeless, indivisible,
    changeless, infinite, rested in unconscious dreamless
    sleep,
    And other than the Eternal Parent there was naught,
    either real or apparent.

2. The Germ within the Cosmic Egg takes unto itself
    Form.
    The Flame is re-kindled.
    A Thing exists. Time begins.
    The Pairs of Opposites spring into being.
    The World Soul is born and wakens into
    manifestation.
    The first rays of the new cosmic day break over the
    horizon.
    The One Became Two,
    The Neuter became bi-sexual.
    Two-in-One evolved from the Neuter.
    Generation began.

3. The One becomes many,
    The unity becomes diversity,
    The identical becomes variety.

4. Yet the many remains the one.
    Diversity remains unity,
    Variety remains Identical.

5. The One is the Flame of Life,
   The Many are the sparks in the Flame.
   The Fire, once kindled, kindles everything within its
       sphere;
   The Fire is in everything and everywhere,
   And there is nothing dark or cold within its sphere.

6. As Life is the essence of Spirit,
   So Consciousness is the essence of Life.
   Spirit is one, yet it manifests in many forms of Life.
   Life is one, yet it manifests in many forms of
       Consciousness.
   All Consciousness manifests on seven planes.

7. From the subliminal to the transcendental,
   From that which is, to that which was,
   And God requireth that which was.
   For the All is One and all are part,
   And not apart as they seem to be.
   And the blood of life has a single heart,
   Beating through God, and clod, and thee.

The Seven Aphorisms form the mythic or poetic basis for a detailed series of lectures on cosmology and esoteric principles, which Moriarty collected together and had privately published, some thirty years after he had first delivered the verses and lectures to his small group of pupils. The quotation above is from this private collection. While no one would pretend that these verses are great poetry, they provided a vehicle for further exposition, and represent an attempt to encapsulate esoteric comprehension of creation into a concise traditional form. The highly concentrated and gnomic verse tradition for creation mythology reaches back into the most distant history of humankind and the *Aphorisms of Creation* are clearly intended to be in the great tradition of mystical and metaphysical verses.

APPENDIX 2:

GENESIS

Having summarised, demonstrated and discussed the patterns inherent within creation mythology, we may now without further commentary quote from the text of one of the creation myths inherent in the Christian religion, based upon Jewish sacred texts; many aspects of the creation traditions in these Jewish texts may be traced back to those of ancient Babylon and Assyria, as known from archaeological evidence. The following extract is from the King James revised translation.

GENESIS: CHAPTER I

1. In the beginning God created the heaven and the earth.

2. And the earth was waste and void and darkness was upon the face of the deep; and the spirit of God moved upon the face of the waters.

3. And God said, Let there be light; and there was light.

4. And God saw the light, that it was good; and God divided the light from the darkness.

5. And God called the light Day, and the darkness he called Night. And there was evening, and there was morning, one day.

6. And God said, Let there be a firmament in the midst of the waters, and Let it divide the waters from the waters.

7. And God made the firmament, and divided the waters which were under the firmament from the waters which were above the firmament; and it was so.

8. And God called the firmament Heaven. And there was evening and there was morning, a second day.

9. And God said, Let the waters under the heaven be gathered together unto one place, and let the dry land appear; and it was so.

10. And God called the dry land earth; and the gathering together of the waters called he seas; and God saw that it was good.

11. And God said, Let the earth put forth grass, herb yielding seed, fruit tree bearing fruit after its kind, wherein is the seed thereof, upon the earth; and it was so.

12. And the earth brought forth grass, herb yielding seed after its kind, and tree bearing fruit, wherein is the seed thereof, after its kind: and God saw that it was good.

13. And there was evening and there was morning, a third day.

14. And God said, Let there be lights in the firmament of the heaven, to divide the day from the night; and let them be for signs and for seasons, and for days and years;

15. And let them be for lights in the heaven to give light upon the earth; and it was so.

16. And God made the two great lights: the greater light to rule the day, and the lesser light to rule the night; he made the stars also.

17. And God set them in the firmament of the heaven to give light upon the earth,

18. And to rule over the day and over the night, and to divide the light from the darkness; and God saw that it was good.

SELECT
BIBLIOGRAPHY

This short bibliography offers a general selection of books for further reading; some are very general titles, others are specific source texts. This list is not detailed in an academic sense, as it crosses over the boundaries of various disciplines and arts which are broadly related to the subjects of cosmology, mythology, meditation, and the imagination. It is intended as a guide to books covering subjects outlined in our preceding chapters. All of the titles listed carry detailed bibliographies for further study.

Branston, Brian *Gods of the North* Thames and Hudson, London.

Branston, B. *The Lost Gods of England* Thames and Hudson, London.

Cotterell, A. *A Dictionary of World Mythology* Book Club Associates, London.

De Santillana, G. & Von Dechend, H. *Hamlet's Mill* Godine.

Dhiravamsa, V.R. *The Way of Non-Attachment* Crucible, Wellingborough.

Evans-Wentz, W.Y. *The Tibetan Book of The Dead* Oxford University Press.

Fell, B. *America B.C.* Pocket Books, New York.

Frazer, Sir James, *The Golden Bough* MacMillan, London.

Ginsburg, Christian, D. *The Essenes* and *The Kabbalah* Routledge and Kegan Paul, London.

Govinda, A. *Foundations of Tibetan Mysticism* Rider, London.

Graham-Campbell, J. *The Viking World* Book Club Associates, London.

Graves, R. *The Greek Myths* Penguin, Harmondsworth.

Hesiod *The Theogony* (various translations).

Holmberg, U. *'Finno-Ugric Mythology'* in *The Mythology of All Races* Vol.4, Harrap, London.

Homer *The Iliad & The Odyssey* (various translations).

James, E.O. *Prehistoric Religion* Thames and Hudson, London.

John, L. (Ed) *Cosmology Now* BBC Publications, London.

Kaplan, A. *Meditation and Kabbalah* Weiser, New York.

Kaplan, Aryeh, *Meditation and the Bible* Samuel Weiser, Inc., New York.

Kendrick, T. *The Druids* Methuen, London.

Lloyd, G.E.R. *'Plato as a natural scientist'* in *The Journal of Hellenic Studies* Vol. LXXXVIII, London.

MacCulloch, J.A. *The Celtic and Scandinavian Religions* Hutchinson's University Library, London.

MacGregor Mathers, S.L. (trans): *The Kabbalah Unveiled* 13th impression, Routledge and Kegan Paul, London.

Matthews, C. & J., *The Aquarian Guide to British and Irish Mythology* Aquarian Press, Wellingborough.

Mead, G.R.S. *Quests Old and New* G Bell & Sons, London.

Müller, M. *'Zend Avesta'* in *Sacred Books of the East* Vol. 23, Clarendon Press, Oxford.

Myers, F.J. *The Unknown God* Thomas's Publications Ltd, Birmingham.

Oesterley, W. & Robinson, T. *Hebrew Religion* SPCK, London.

Plato *The Republic* (various translations).

Pritchard, J. *Ancient Near Eastern Texts relating to the Old Testament* Oxford University Press.

Purce, J. *The Mystic Spiral* Thames and Hudson, London.

Rees, A. & B. *Celtic Heritage* Thames and Hudson, London.

Rose, H. *A handbook of Greek Mythology* Methuen, London.

Ross, A. *Pagan Celtic Britain* Cardinal, London.

Spence, L. *The Myths of the North American Indians* Harrap, London.

Spence, L. *The Occult Sciences in Atlantis* Aquarian Press, Wellingborough.

Sperling, Harry and Simon, Maurice (trans): *The Zohar* Vol. 1, Soncino Press, London.

Steiner, R. *Knowledge of the Higher Worlds* Steiner Publishing Co, London.

Stewart, R.J. *Advanced Magical Arts* Element Books, Shaftesbury.

Stewart, R.J. *Celtic Gods and Goddesses* Blandford Press, London.

Stewart, R.J. *Living Magical Arts* Blandford Press, Poole.

Stewart R.J. *Music and the Elemental Psyche* Aquarian Press, Wellingborough.

Stewart, R.J. *The Merlin Tarot* (Book and full colour deck of cards illustrated by Miranda Gray) Aquarian Press, Wellingborough.

Stewart, R.J. *The Mystic Life of Merlin* Penguin, Arkana, Harmondsworth.

Stewart, R.J. *The Prophetic Vision of Merlin* Penguin, Arkana, Harmondsworth.

Stewart, R.J. *The Underworld Initiation* Aquarian Press, Wellingborough.

Stewart, R.J. & Matthews, J. *Legendary Britain* Blandford Press, London.

Stewart, R.J. & Matthews, J. *Warriors of Arthur* Blandford Press, London.

Stirling, W. *The Canon* Research Into Lost Knowledge Organisation, London.

Velikovsky, I. *Worlds in Collision* Abacus, London.

Wind, E. *Pagan Mysteries in the Renaissance* Oxford University Press.

Winston, David (trans): *Philo of Alexandria* SPCK, London.

Wynn Westcott, W. (trans): *The Sepher Yetzirah and The Thirty Two Paths of Wisdom* Samuel Weiser, Inc., New York (undated modern reprint of 19th century edition).

Yates, F. *The Art of Memory* Routledge and Kegan Paul, London.

Young, J. *The Prose Edda* Bowes, London.

INDEX